Credit and Sales:

THE WINNING TEAM

Lynn Tylczak

National Association of Credit Management
Publications Department
8815 Centre Park Drive, Suite 200
Columbia, Maryland 21045-2158

ISBN 0-934914-89-3

Printed in the United States of America

Editor: Teresa Donohue, NACM
Page Design & Composition: Christine Rees, NACM
Cover Design: Chris Quinn Graphic Design
Typeface: 11/13.5 Times Roman
Printing: McNaughton & Gunn

Contents

Introduction

It is natural for sales professionals like yourself to think of your company's credit and collection department as a thwart, rather than a support service. As one frustrated high tech salesperson put it, "My job is to bring in the business. The credit manager's job is to send it away."

In truth, your credit and collection cohorts have the same primary function you do: to maximize corporate profits. Obviously, that's easier said than done. The risks and rewards inherent in dealing with prospective purchasers, new businesses, marginal accounts and cash-poor companies can make credit calls as tough as cold calls.

This book isn't about sales and it isn't about credit. It's about synergy: how to add one (you) and one (a supportive credit and collection counterpart) to get three times the sales. It's about creating a credit/sales interface whose sum total is greater in value than the value of its individual parts.

This book will show you how to use credit as a sales tool to speed credit approvals, successfully gather confidential financial/business information, maintain profitable accounts and circumvent potential profit problems. In other words, you'll learn new techniques for boosting your company's bottom line.

If you want a helping hand in today's tough business environment, don't bite the hand that helps to feed you sales. Remember, by making it easier for prospects to buy, your credit department makes it easier for you to sell.

Chapter 1

The Interdependence of Sales and Credit

Salespeople survive according to the law of the jungle. It's a dog-eat-dog business world.

But when the sales and credit departments interact, a different law rules. Perhaps you've heard of it. Murphy's Law: "Anything that can go wrong, will."

Perhaps one of the following examples has even happened to you:

Example #1: You work for months to line up a new account, and what happens? Your credit manager refuses to grant the prospect a line of credit and offers the buyer terms of sale—say, C.O.D. or 50 percent now, 50 percent upon delivery—that are hardly terms of endearment. In doing so, the credit manager terminates your hard-won purchase order.

You lose three ways. You lose the past: the time and effort you've already invested in this prospect (and could have invested more profitably elsewhere). You lose the present: the initial purchase order and its related commission. And, worst of all, you lose the future—all those down-the-line-dollars you would have received if this present prospect had become a continuing customer. Three strikes and you're out—out a lot of money.

Example #2: You have a long-term account, a customer so established that you almost think of his purchase commissions as a sort of annuity. You've sent materials to him, and he's sent checks to your company, for years. You (and your credit department comrades) have always considered him a great credit risk.

Suddenly, for unspecified reasons, the credit department decides that the customer is too great a credit risk. They turn off his credit, and as a result, he turns away all of your subsequent sales overtures.

Example #3: You have a major buyer who unexpectedly becomes a major victim of its business environment. Perhaps it declares bankruptcy or is the target of a hostile takeover. In the first instance, you'll have to deal with attorneys and the bankruptcy court; in the second, you'll find yourself facing preoccupied ("I can't bother with that now") purchasers.

In either scenario you can expect to see both commission and collection complications.

Example #4: The reigning credit staff decide (with good reason) to tighten the credit reins. First, they fiddle with the fast-pay discount. They impose a new, tighter timeline, making it impossible for many customers to receive the desired discount. They decrease the discount amount, making the deal much less ideal. They start disallowing any discounts taken after the decided deadline (something they should have done all along), irritating past due penny pinchers.

Second, the credit department increases interest charges on past due accounts, upsetting the companies that can't always pay up.[1] The new minimum interest charges (say, $10 a month) horrify minimal buyers ("A $20 interest charge on a $25 invoice?"). Instead of charging interest only after the account is 30 days past due, they start accruing interest on the third day.

Third, the credit staff suddenly seek quarterly financial statements and credit reports, even from long-term customers. They start insisting on personal guarantees, personnel information and co-signatories.

Sure, the credit department staff have good reason for requiring said changes, but their insistence generates customer resistance. Unfortunately, when customers and credit staffers don't meet eye to eye, it isn't long before customers start meeting with competitors. And where does that leave you?

Example #5: For years you've fought head to head with Competitor X, but now he's trying to fight pocketbook to pocketbook. His plan: to use credit terms to differentiate his product.

Your product lines are competitive in terms of price, quality, functionality and desirability. As far as the customer is concerned, they

[1] Most companies indicate in their credit contracts that they can and/or will charge interest on past due accounts. It still upsets customers when they see it for the first time (particularly if it's a new corporate practice).

appear equal. Competitor X suddenly offers the customer a 5 percent fast-pay discount, no interest for 12 months, or an astronomical credit limit. You offer your company's standard financial fare (2 percent discount, 18 percent interest on all past due accounts and reasonable credit limits). You're suddenly without a customer.

Unfortunately, these practical applications of Murphy's Law aren't uncommon occurrences. Ask anyone in sales and they'll tell you that credit crises are SOP—a Standard Occupational Problem.

When credit concerns create customer chaos, it's natural to want to blame someone. Sometimes, if the salesperson is being honest with himself, he'll acknowledge that he's the one who dropped the ball ("I thought something fishy was going on at ABC, but I was too busy to call our credit manager."). Sometimes, it's the credit department that was behind the eight ball ("The credit department didn't tell me that DEF was 60 days past due, so I kept processing its orders"). Sometimes a ball comes out of left field and nobody has a chance to see it coming ("How were we supposed to know the parent company was going to pull the plug on its unprofitable infant?").

Blame, of course, is counterproductive. Delegating guilt doesn't solve the problem or save your sales. What's needed is productive, profit-oriented problem solving.

The Three C's of Credit and Beyond

Experienced money managers base their credit decisions on what is commonly called the "three C's" of credit: character, capacity and capital. Basically, what a credit manager wants to know is: "Does the potential customer have the ability to pay its bills?" and "Does this potential customer feel obligated to pay its bills?"

These three C's would be sufficient if credit and collections were totally internal tasks. Clearly, they are not. The credit department provides a support service. To do that effectively, it needs to work closely with its "customers:" the salespeople and, indirectly, the salespeople's customers. It needs more than the traditional "three C's." It needs:

1. **Cooperation**. The credit department and the sales staff must be willing to work together for the common corporate good. In some instances, that means extending credit; in others, it means ending credit. It always means working together.

The credit and sales departments are interdependent. Without sales, there is no need for a credit department. Without a credit department, making it possible for customers to buy, there is no need for salespeople. In short, the interdependence may be uncomfortable, but you can't live without it.

2. **Communication**. The credit and the sales staff must actively share account information. Communication works both ways. Nobody likes or deserves unpleasant surprises.

If your credit counterparts are going to derail a customer's credit line, they need to drop you a line first. This gives you a chance to prepare and propose payment alternatives, possibly allowing the customer to save face and you to save the account.

Conversely, if you're aware of any negative knowledge, you need to pass it on to your credit colleagues. If they subsequently decide to pass on the account, you can bet it's for a good reason.

Always, the common denominator is the common corporate good. The credit and sales staffs both work to maximize profitable sales.[2]

3. **Courtesy**. Courtesy also runs both ways in a well run credit/sales interface. You must treat the other party as you would like to be treated (or mistreated). Respect is required, and give and take is essential. Losing a past due amount is at least as painful as losing a promising new account.

Credit and sales positions are both tough jobs. Working together, rather than merely co-existing, can help both parties tough it out.

This book isn't really about credit. It's about sales. Your company's sales. If you can make cooperation, communication and courtesy part of your game plan, you can plan on making more money. It's all in the attitude. Credit and sales forces unite: We're all in this together. United we stand, divided our corporate profits fall.

Sales and Credit Functions

If the credit and sales departments are going to stand together, they each need to know where they stand relative to the other department's functions.

[2] Sales, of course, is defined as a "transfer of goods for payment" (as opposed to unintentional "charitable donations," which is what you have when buyers can't or won't pay for the goods they receive).

Consider the sales side of the equation. As leaders of the profit pack, salespeople have to score big bucks while carrying the ball for the sideline squads (advertising, marketing, manufacturing, distribution, etc.). The result is a team effort with sales at the forefront.

Unfortunately, some team members—namely the credit squad—may not be viewed as team players. Why? Their decisions can debilitate, rather than facilitate, a salesperson's profit-building game plan. He may find himself wondering, "Just whose side is the credit department on?" Things can turn ugly.

For example, let's say you want to sell your product line, on credit, to ABC. Based on ABC's character/capital/capacity, your credit department refuses to offer it a credit line, even one containing the most token of terms. They will not give credit where you think credit is due.

While this edict may be a good credit decision, it may also be a bad business decision. The strategic importance of ABC's business to you, your marketing program and your company's profits and goals, may outweigh the obvious credit risk.

Making Balanced, Informed Credit Decisions

When making its credit decisions, the credit department could have overlooked (or may not have been told) how important ABC's business is to the company's distribution plans. For example, having ABC for a client will help you and your company build distribution in a previously under-serviced geographic area. Having ABC for a client will help build distribution in a previously untapped market (e.g., you've always sold your product to contractor-only electrical supply stores, ABC is a do-it-yourself, home improvement center). Adding ABC to your current clients will minimize aggregate shipping expenses and maximize shipping efficiency.

Perhaps the credit department was unaware of how ABC's business would affect the manufacturing department. ABC may be willing to purchase hard-to-move, still-around stock (factory seconds, overstocks, unclaimed custom or special orders, or closeouts). ABC may be willing to purchase inventory during the off-season, making it easier to manage manufacturing and smooth sales slumps. ABC may be willing to create a strategic manufacturing alliance or share proprietary production information.

Then there's the unaddressed advertising/marketing component. ABC may, through co-op advertising, point-of-purchase displays, piggybacking, or mere association, significantly increase your brand's desirability/recognition (this can increase sales both to end users and to ABC's competitors, who may want to carry the same name brands). Maybe ABC, unlike the other outlets in its market or area, is willing to carry your entire line (and you can use ABC's actions to convince other more reluctant buyers to do the same).

The credit department probably wasn't given the complete profit picture. Overall, ABC may be a relatively inexpensive account to service. It may be interested in purchasing only the most profitable products. ABC may have substantial influence over critical end users, enough to help you sell profitable ancillary services such as product options, upgrades or long-term maintenance contracts.

It's also possible that ABC's purchases would increase your profit margins by decreasing unit costs (e.g., it's cheaper, on a per unit basis, to make 10,000 manufactured items than it is to make 100). Another important consideration: ABC may be about to hit the sales stratosphere (e.g., it just received a valuable distribution or sales contract, lost its major competitor, licensed a valuable patent, or is receiving lots of favorable press) and you could hitch your wagon to a rising star.

When customers like ABC hang in the balance, balanced business decisions are necessary. Balanced business decisions are a product of informed credit decisions. Informed credit decisions are the norm when the credit department is aware of both credit and strategic sales information.

The credit department is aware of both credit and strategic sales information when the sales staff practices the "three C's:" **cooperation** ("How can we work together to help this prospect buy our product?"), **communication** ("These are the reasons why this customer is worth the credit risk..."), and **courtesy** ("I respect your professional opinion. Would you change your mind about granting credit to this customer if..."). It is the three C criteria which ensure that the sales/credit interface is constructive rather than destructive, profitable rather than problematic.

Selling is a relatively easy function to understand: find the need, fill the need, you succeed.[3] The basis of credit and collections—determining if a prospect is willing and able to pay for credit purchases—is a

[3] Although, like most professional tasks, it is easier done than said.

little more complicated. There are more variables to contaminate considerations. Still, if salespeople are going to work profitably with their credit colleagues, they need to understand the credit profession's parameters and constraints.

It's difficult being a credit and collections professional, because people love what you control (credit) and hate the fact that you must control it.

The Necessity of Credit

Everybody loves credit. They might as well: credit is both a business and an economic necessity. There simply isn't enough cash to run a currency-only economy. Even people who think they run their businesses on a cash-and-carry basis sometimes find themselves unexpectedly carrying bad debts (otherwise known as bad checks).

Customers love supplier-supplied credit. It's convenient, and it sure beats sending cash through the mail or keeping bags of bills on the premises. Supplier credit is less expensive, more readily available, and more forgiving than bank lines of credit. Credit generates managerial control by creating an auditable paper trail; it facilitates financial control by allowing CFOs to decide when to pay, how much to pay, and whom to pay (not to mention what to do with the money in the meantime).

The use of credit ensures good customer service ("Pay attention to my concerns or I won't pay attention to your bills"). It boosts the buyer's business ego (they're sending me merchandise on faith because they have faith in me). And, probably its most important asset: credit allows a customer to procure your product while procrastinating his payment.

Because buyers love credit, suppliers love credit. Suppliers commonly use credit to meet a number of objectives. Credit can create sales (ever hear of installment plans?). Credit can improve profit margins by allowing suppliers to charge more for their products (yes, the products cost more, but when purchased on credit, they're still affordable). Credit makes it possible to access can't-pay-cash customers (governmental organizations, big businesses, cash-poor prospects).

Companies often use credit to differentiate their deals ("we offer better payment terms than our competitors") and strengthen customer loyalty. Credit clearly creates a positive company image ("we offer credit because we're successful and we can afford to"). Finally, when you give a customer access to credit, you're giving something the customer both wants and needs. That's what successful sales is all about.

Unfortunately, every silver lining has a cloud. It's sometimes necessary for the credit department to rain on the sales staff's purchase order parade. After all, credit staffers are in charge of, and responsible for, a challenging charge. It's not a job for the faint-hearted.

The fact is, credit is both a dangerous and an expensive proposition. Every year, billions of dollars are lost to bad credit decisions and payment procrastination. One credit rule of thumb states that past due accounts are 10 percent uncollectible after 60 days, 33-67 percent uncollectible after 6 months, and 55-78 percent uncollectible after one year. Another statistic indicates that based on account collectibility, $1 is worth only 94 cents after 30 days, 85 cents after 60 days, 74 cents after 90 days, 58 cents after 6 months, 43 cents after 9 months, 27 cents after 12 months, 14 cents after 2 years.

And other credit realities rear their ugly heads. The company can only carry so many customers. There is a limit as to how much credit any company can give (or get). If a company's money is tied up in carrying past due customers, it can't fully service its current accounts.

Credit staffers have limited information on which to make their credit decisions. What they'd like to have is a year's worth of financial statements (at least one of them audited), a current credit report, a list of outstanding financial guarantees/ commitments, and five high-quality business references. What they usually get is the standard credit report (which, depending on the credit reporting company, could be more than a year old) and a few references that the prospect can count on. And, what they occasionally get is set up by a finely-tuned fraud.

To keep up with its corporate customers, credit staffers have to keep up with the times. Even firmly-controlled firms are in a constant state of financial flux. A customer that was a good risk yesterday may be a big risk today. Perhaps its growth is slowing or its competitors are growing. Maybe it was so creditworthy that it got more credit than it deserved. Too many suppliers offered too much credit, and it took on too much debt. A change in top management may also necessitate a change in credit limits, particularly if the outstanding balance was guaranteed by the past principals.

Credit staffers are often put in impossible positions. They are expected to collect past due accounts without alienating careless-with-credit customers. They're asked to grant instant credit approval without any fiduciary perusal. Major advertising or marketing campaigns are often designed with no consideration given to the additional burden placed upon the credit staff. They're commonly accused of obstructing, rather than constructing, purchases when all they've done is their job. When it comes to granting credit, they're damned if they allow the customer to become past due, and damned if they don't.

Obviously, the roles of the salesperson and credit manager are—and need to be—as different as night and day. As a salesperson, you aren't expected to see things through the jaundiced eye of the credit professional, just as the credit staffer isn't supposed to see things through the rose-colored glasses of the ever-optimistic salesperson. It would help, however, if both parties could see the other party's views. The way to develop credit-conscious salespeople and sales-sensitive credit people is by practicing cooperation, communication and courtesy.

Working together, salespeople and credit managers can find ways to increase sales while minimizing risk. They can be problem solvers, not trouble makers. They can replace traditional "yes/no" credit decisions with the more powerful "Yes, if..." In short, they can maximize corporate profits without minimizing the other party.

Chapter 2

Promoting the New or Potential Buyer

In some professions, a person can coast and still get ahead. It's a function of Newton's second law: bodies (or careers!) in motion tend to stay in motion.

That law doesn't apply to people in the sales profession. A salesperson doesn't dare coast—even when the coast is clear of competitors. In sales, you have to keep running just to stay even. Again, the problem is Newton's second law. Bodies in motion—this time, bodies of buyers—tend to stay in motion. Much of this motion involves moving in and out of current account lists, moving from one supplier to another, moving from one product or technology to another.

Account Attrition and the Changing Customer

Even carefully cultivated customers will occasionally leave your care. There are a variety of good (and not so good!) reasons for this rollover, but all of the reasons are related in one respect: they are a function, a manifestation, of change.

Some customers will stop purchasing your products because their status changes. They go out of business, vanishing into thin air. Or they go out of their own business and into a merger/acquisition mayhem. They become holding companies or are themselves held by ESOPs. They are held captive by Chapter 7 or Chapter 11 proceedings. They change from a single proprietorship with a financially set owner to an underfunded corporation. They need less product because, thanks to downsized divisions, there are fewer internal customers to service. Or perhaps the customer has grown large enough to manufacture components in-house (or in one of its new overseas facilities). In short, when a company changes its status, it also changes its purchasing status quo.

Other accounts will drop off or disappear because of changes relative to the people parameter. A change in ownership often precipitates a change in purchasing practices (this is even true when a family business is passed from one generation to another). Credit lines may disappear with an old owner's financial guarantees or business expertise. New partners or purchasing agents can disrupt old customer loyalties (i.e., when new purchasers move in, they tend to bring their prior purchasing relationships with them).

Customers are often lost when their specific needs or wants change. You may find your company unable to accommodate these new needs. For example, a current customer may dictate an untenable technological timeline. Or, it may turn its purchasing procedures upside down, perhaps moving from centralized to decentralized purchasing practices.

You may also find your territory torn apart by rapidly changing values. Customers may start focusing on cost rather than quality, on availability instead of exclusivity, on state-of-the-art technologies as opposed to good-enough gadgets. Distribution channels may rechannel your customers' interest. For example, in the late 1980s many business buyers stopped purchasing their stationery supplies from service-oriented specialty shops and began buying from price-pushing, volume-oriented, discount dealers. It's clear: When buyers rechannel their purchasing, the salesperson must also change channels.

Account attrition is a way of life. Fortunately, there's a way to overcome its negative revenue repercussions. All you need to do is *get new customers*. If you think that's easier said than done, you're right. But if you take the global view, you'll also see that it's easier to do than it sounds. After all, one salesperson's loss is another's gain. Business doesn't totally dry up and blow away; what you see is a shift in its weather patterns (whether to buy from X or Y). For every salesperson who's parched of purchase orders, there's a competitor who's flooded with business.

The same business balance holds true for customers. For every business that goes broke, there are unbroken competitors (perhaps even new businesses) that need more product to fill that business's void. In every purchasing shift, there is a chance for some salesperson to shift gears, to move with the purchaser, and to initiate sales via a new account. Business needs evolve, but not beyond the need for outside products. Businesses will always have to buy something.

The ultimate challenge in lining up new customers is in getting a line on their purchasing power. This task is never easy since so much is at stake: sales, profitability, market share, etc. It's serious business. Prospects must be handled with kid gloves.

There are two types of sales prospects: the new-to-you customers and the new-to-view customers. Because they are relatively unknown quantities, both will unavoidably generate large quantities of credit department concern.

The New-to-You Customer

New-to-you customers are established buyers who have established their credit histories with other firms. Perhaps they previously purchased their products from a competitor, or are entering a new entrepreneurial enclave. They've been around for a while, they just haven't gotten around to buying from you. In other words, they are a going concern and, as such, wouldn't appear to cause much credit department concern.

You may be assuming (correctly) that these new-to-you firms are sound, but here's a word to the wise. Even a long-term firm may not be what it first appears to be. For example, the much-pursued prospect you just wooed away from a close competitor may have left with no love lost. Perhaps it started buying from you because it had worn out its credit welcome at your competitors. Perhaps, instead of running *to* you, it is actually running *away from* your competitor's collection department. If that's the case, it's no prize prospect. You'd be advised to stay well away.

An old (but new-to-you) firm entering a new field may also field new credit problems. It's relatively easy to predict a firm's creditworthiness as long as it stands firm. But what happens when it intentionally shakes itself up, when it virtually reinvents its business? It may not truly understand the nature of, nor the risks involved in, its new opportunity. What happens if the "new and improved" company can't make a go of it and, subsequently, can't pay its bills? What if the opportunity costs are higher, and the revenues lower, than the floundering firm positively projected? Again, an old, established (but new-to-you) business that appears to be a solid risk can quickly dissolve into credit quicksand.

The New-to-View Customer

New-to-view prospects present the greatest credit risk of all. These business buyers are new—at least in their present incarnation—to everyone. They have no credit history; they may have no history of any kind. What qualifies as a new-to-view prospect? The definition is broader than you might think.

A company that just opened its doors (or whose doors are still under construction) would be considered a new-to-view. So would a previously pampered departmental dynasty that was suddenly set loose as a self-financing subsidiary, or a proprietary progeny that a parent company recently sold to the highest bidder. These two spin-offs would not be new *to* the business, but they would certainly be new *as* a business and would have to be treated as such. An old established company that, due to a change in ownership (and a loss of co-signatories/financial guarantees, character, reputation, etc.) has to start anew in building its corporate credibility, would also be a new-to-view. If the company is, in any major sense, "new and improved" it is invariably a new-to-view.

The risks inherent in new-to-view prospects are clear. There is no way to accurately use the "three C's" of credit. There is no corporate character to assess because the business hasn't had time to build a purchasing or payment personality. There is questionable capacity, given that the firm in question is still in its industrial infancy. The ability to service a debt is largely a function of cash flow, and predicting the cash flow of new businesses is virtually impossible.[4] And capital? Have you ever seen an over-capitalized new business?

[4]One study found that 93 percent of all new businesses drastically overestimated their predicted revenues for their first three years in business. Why assume that other people—people who know less about the new company's organizational structure, management expertise, product, advertising/marketing/sales plans and personal/professional contacts—do much better?

The long and short of it is, it's risky to sign up new customers, but it's more risky not to. Avoiding new-to-you or new-to-view businesses is not technically a risk. It's a sure thing, a sure sign that your business will eventually die. Customer attrition inevitably will bleed you dry.

If you plan on maintaining—let alone increasing—your sales, you need to fight account attrition with account addition. You must add new accounts to make up for those you will inevitably (unfortunately) lose. You'll want to work with the credit and collections department so that the process is as painless and as profitable as possible.

The Ten New-Credit Commandments

You can simultaneously serve your new purchasing prospects and your credit and collections system. All you have to do is follow the Ten New-Credit Commandments.

1. Ask your credit department to conduct a pre-sale credit check on every prospect before you make your initial contact. Let them invest time and money in credit research before you invest time and money in sales calls.

Think about it: you wouldn't consider selling chainsaws or industrial solvents to a child care center. And, you wouldn't waste time trying to sell tulip bulbs or fine faceted gems to a carpet wholesaler. Assuming that you could even close these sales, would you want them? The answer, of course, is no. You don't sell merchandise just to sell merchandise. You sell products to customers because they satisfy a customer's particular needs and wants.

The key phrase is "customer needs and wants." Supplier credit is as legitimate a customer need/want as product quality, low prices, or turnkey delivery schedules. Some customers will only buy the very best. Some customers will only buy the very cheapest. Some customers will only buy from the very fastest firms. And, unfortunately, there are those customers who will never vary and insist that they will only (or can only) buy from a firm that will grant them liberal credit/payment terms.

If your company can't or won't offer acceptable credit terms to a credit-needy prospect, then you may lose the sale because you cannot meet one of your prospect's basic needs/wants.

The Advantages of Pre-Sale Credit Checks

If you're like most salespeople, you've probably spent a great deal of time, money and effort pursuing that prospect who could (for credit reasons) never become a customer. Fortunately, this is an easy problem to solve. Simply have your credit department investigate each prospect's credit potential before you invest your resources. An inexpensive, skim-the-surface, preliminary credit check should ensure that you only pursue prospects that are worth catching.

The advantages for both you and your buyer are enormous. From the prospect's point of view, you aren't wasting its time with wishful-thinking product presentations ("we'd love those but we can't afford them"). You aren't laying waste to its organizational ego ("we could sell this to you if you had more 'character'"). Put yourself in the prospect's shoes. It's embarrassing to be pursued by salespeople, but rejected by their credit departments. Making prospects feel this way is bad for business.

From a sales perspective, pre-purchase credit checks offer numerous benefits. As suggested earlier, they ensure that you aren't wasting your time, money and effort on unqualified buyers. Used properly, they will help you direct your resources toward more profitable prospects (or current customers). In short, they help you maximize your means.

You can use pre-purchase credit checks to support your initial sales presentation. They work well as a closing tool ("Since your company has a pre-approved credit line of $5,000, we can process this purchase order today"). Preliminary checks can be packaged as a sales benefit ("we have convenient, one-stop, product-and-credit shopping"). They demonstrate to your customers that you're on the ball and can get the business ball rolling. Not surprisingly, pre-purchase credit checks are popular with customers because immediate credit means instant purchasing power.

Pre-purchase credit checks can circumvent potentially embarrassing situations. For example, if a prospect's pre-sales credit check indicates unavoidable problems, you won't be tempted to offer it an unattainable credit line. If requested by the credit department, you can ask the prospect for financial statements or other credit information before the first sale is sewn up. Done early, your request will look routine, rather than reactionary.

Thanks to pre-sale credit checks, you and your credit colleagues can generate credit decisions and offer options ("we will offer Prospect A a credit line of $10,000 if...") in an objective and professional manner before a solid sale is at stake. You will feel more confident about closing the prospect's first purchase because certain credit decisions have already been made.

Pre-sale credit checks make it possible for you to approve spur-of-the-moment sales and unexpected rush orders. Let's say you've been trying to recruit Prospect XYZ for a number of months. As part of this process, you've had a preliminary credit check run and have been given the authority to offer it a $5000 initial line of credit.

You get your first sale to XYZ because you happened to be in the right place at the right time to write up an important rush order. You got your foot in the door because XYZ had the door open, looking for the nearest available salesperson. That is, XYZ was looking for the nearest available salesperson who could write up a rush order and extend enough credit to cover it.

Now consider what would have happened if you had approached XYZ without a pre-sale credit check in hand. Any proffered purchase order has to come with cash or be contingent upon a credit decision. If XYZ needs its order ASAP and it needs credit as part of the purchase, it's going to be difficult—if not impossible—to seal the sale.[5] It takes time, more time than is allowed by most rush orders, to determine a company's credit-quantifying character, capacity and capital.

Bottomline: You have to successfully process XYZ's first (albeit rush) purchase or you'll never get another. Why? Because if you don't deliver, the buyer's first (and lasting) impression of you is going to be that it handed you a sale and you couldn't or wouldn't handle it. In short, your future sales success often depends on your past pre-sale practices.

[5] Rush orders are no problem for the credit department. Rush credit decisions are another matter. Credit information isn't always readily available, and much of the easy-to-access information is likely to be of questionable origin. A prospect, for example, is only going to give your company good credit references. It takes more time (and money) to find less flattering and/or more factual feedback because your prospect isn't going to help you look.

In addition, it's important to remember that an inordinate number of rush orders are fraudulent. A good pre-sale credit check will help determine if the prospect has a checkered past.

Here's more good news: Pre-purchase credit checks are as popular with credit departments as they are with successful salespeople. The reason is simple. Time is money, and unfortunately your credit comrades never have enough of this valuable commodity. There's never enough time to make good credit decisions. There's always enough time—and sufficient sales pressure—to make bad ones.

Bad credit decisions lead to both lost customers and high-cost customers. Some customers are lost because, without credit research, your credit department doesn't dare give them credit. Others generate high costs because, without sufficient credit information, your credit department isn't able to positively pinpoint those prospects who will need to be pursued for payments.

Bad credit decisions are usually a result of bad timing, of unrealistic deadline pressures. You can prevent this perpetual problem by requesting pre-sale credit checks. This makes it possible for your credit and collections department to generate good data and calibrate profitable decisions.[6]

Make pre-sale credit checks a part of your sales strategy checklist. If you give your credit department the research time it needs, it will give you the sales support you need. Together, you'll achieve the common goal of increased corporate profits. You'll make more sales, and the credit department will make better use of corporate funds.

2. Provide complete and accurate prospect information to the credit department whenever you request a pre-sale credit check. Without it, your colleagues may very well investigate the wrong party.

The more complete, accurate and relevant the information given by the salesperson, the better (the less risky and more profitable) the credit decision. When the credit department has all the information it needs, it's likely to go down the correct path.

In reality, your credit department needs only three pieces of information to begin a pre-sale credit check: the company's legal name ("The

[6] Given time, your credit department can gather most of the credit information it needs through the mail. The postal process has two major benefits. First, requesting and receiving data by mail can be a lot less expensive than similar telephone/fax research. Second, receiving financial data via the U.S. Postal Service reduces the probability of fraud (attempting to secure credit by sending fraudulent financial information through the U.S. mail is a federal offense).

ABC Company" rather than "ABC"), the complete company address, and the names of the corporate owners, officers and/or registered agents. These shouldn't be difficult to ascertain (presumably you aren't addressing the prospect by the wrong name or in the wrong places), but they are certainly critical to the credit department.

Get the Company Name Right

If you provide your credit department with an incorrect or incomplete company name, you can create two possible problems. First, your credit department may do a pre-sale credit check on the wrong company. Gems Inc., Gems Ink, and Gem Zinc have similar names but they will each have unique credit histories.

Second, if your credit department begins its research with the wrong company name, it will find itself on a wild goose chase. That wastes time, money and the cooperative spirit. All of this can be avoided if you simply make sure you communicate the correct company name.

It's also important to remember that many businesses intentionally choose names that are similar to those of currently successful corporations.[7] Sometimes, this is done because imitation is the sincerest form of flattery (whether the inspiring individual likes it or not).

Sometimes this almost-the-same-name game is played because the copying company wants its suppliers to form a flattering first impression. As one credit manager puts it, "Names mean less than nothing. IBM and I Be M are related alphabetically and phonetically, but not financially or substantially. Mistaking one for the other would be a major mistake."

A Complete Address is Essential

The second piece of information vital to an effective pre-sales credit check is the prospect's complete legal address. Bad addresses are really bad news when it comes to credit research. Let's say you have a sales lead from a prospect on Main Street. Could you find the firm with this

[7] Many companies accidentally choose similar names for their companies or products. In one famous lawsuit, a major American corporation settled out of court after unintentionally giving its new yogurt a name already used by a small western business.

limited information? Perhaps it's possible, if your sales territory covers a very limited locale. But what if you service a multi-metropolitan, multiple-state area? Is your prospect from the Main Street in Albany, Toledo or Portland? And once you've figured that out, are you looking for Albany, New York, or Albany, Arkansas? Toledo, Ohio, or Toledo, Washington? Portland, Maine, or Portland, Oregon? And if it's that difficult for you, knowing your territorial parameters, imagine how hard this geographical guessing game would be for a credit department or a credit reporting company!

Correct prospect addresses are a must because incorrect ones can lead to all sorts of problematic permutations. For example: you need to ensure that the company which is going to receive and pay your invoice is the same company subjected to your pre-sale credit check. Let's say you receive an order from the XYZ Paper holding company in New York. The order is to be delivered and billed to the XYZ Paper subsidiary in Montana. Which XYZ gets the pre-sale credit check? Not the holding company in New York.[8] Not the XYZ Paper subsidiaries in Idaho, North Dakota or South Dakota. Not two other Montana firms, XYZ Paper Products or XYZ Paperweights. Just XYZ Paper of Montana. Or, to be perfectly accurate: XYZ Paper, 100 Main St., Billings, Montana 56789.

"Can't-find-it" complications are undoubtedly detrimental to a credit department. Most credit reporting firms, a primary source of information for the majority of pre-sale credit checks, are national. They don't know your territorial terminology. If you don't supply your credit department with accurate prospect addresses, the credit reporting company may not be able to obtain the information your company needs. The information gathering process will make them feel like they're trying to find a needle in a haystack. They know what they're looking for is in there, but getting their hands on it could be a long and painful process.

Obtain Names of Corporate Managers and Officers

The last piece of information required for the pre-sale credit check is a complete and accurate list of names of the corporate managers, officers

[8] A parent/holding company is not financially responsible for its subsidiaries unless it co-signs the subsidiary's loans. One of the main reasons for spinning off a subsidiary is to make its parent company legally, financially aloof.

and/or registered agents. Gathering such a Who's Who list may seem superfluous to you, but it is necessary to check out a company, its creditworthiness and its potential credit options. The more you know about the people who run the company, the more you know about how the company is likely to be run.

Check Out Companies for Fraud

It's crucial to know who you're dealing with because there may be times when you'll find yourself dealing with a fraud. Knowing the principals involved is one way of identifying a bogus business. Believe it or not, con artists who go from "business" to "business" (that is, from fraud to fraud) will often change their corporate cover (in 1990, it's the ABC Company, in 1991 it's the DEF Company, etc.) but keep their individual identities (every year, the scam is run by good old Jim Jones).

Consider the case of an Alabama convict who defrauded 13,000 companies out of $88 million (before running a $3.5 million fraud from his prison cell). Because sales-conscious companies didn't check out his personal history he was able to abuse their confidence (as indicated by these instructions written to his accomplices on the outside):

"We then order stereos...for immediate shipment. The supplier ships to a public warehouse-freight forwarder, then our trucks pick up their stuff and move it to a secret warehouse...Then we sell to bulk buyers, 500 of these, at a price lower than we paid [for products such as] TVs, VCRs, stereos, all types of computer equipment and software, power tools, home appliances such as microwaves, mixers, dishwashers, pots, pans, knives, luggage, lawn and garden equipment, home furnishings, cameras, jewelry, telephone answering machines, sporting goods...apparel and shoes.

"...Also key to all of this is that the vendors that we deal with are hungry for business and would not even think that anything is wrong.

"...In September, we will have 100 or so vendors slobbering from the mouth, so anxious to 'sell us' they can taste it...You and George will know the ones that are foaming at the mouth to do business with us...Eliminate the ones that you think may cause trouble."[9] (Reprinted

[9] That is, those suppliers who will check out the principals of the organization.

from the National Association of Credit Management, *Business Credit*, July/August 1988 issue, pages 39 and 40).

Thanks to the National Association of Credit Management's Loss Prevention Department, your credit department may quickly research principal and/or company names via a hotline. Surprisingly, in the words of one Loss Prevention staffer, "We have found that a successful bust-out artist will move around the corner or across the street and open up under another name."

Consider the case of John Gurley: "John Gurley, known as the Smokey Mountain Con Man, used to nickel and dime credit departments by placing small, unsolicited orders, generally below the level that would trigger the purchase of a credit report. Hundreds of orders would be placed for amounts ranging from a few hundred to a few thousand dollars. Shipments would be received, no payments made, and then he would close the store, opening up in a nearby Smokey Mountain town a few months later.

"Gurley went to jail for mail fraud when 60 of some 500 companies thought to be his victims provided enough information through the Postal Inspection Service to a federal judge in North Carolina to convince the court of Gurley's intent not to pay." (Reprinted from the National Association of Credit Management, *Business Credit*, March 1988 issue, page 54).

In both of these cases, a case can be made that a pre-sale credit check of the individuals involved would have saved the victims millions of dollars. In any case, it never hurts to know those who could hurt your company.

Note: If your pre-sale credit check indicates that the prospect would be a credit application casualty, having information on the organization's managers/officers/agents will make it possible for your credit department to investigate the possibility of personal guarantees.[10] As a result, what would otherwise have been a corporate credit check/refusal can lead to a personal credit check and an array of credit alternatives.

If you want a meaningful pre-sale credit check, it's no mean feat. All it requires is accurate and complete data relative to the prospect's name, business address and principals. In short, the information you pass on to the credit department has to be more than just passable.

[10] If the prospect doesn't deserve credit, perhaps some of its principals do. If they're willing to co-sign for the company's credit line—and, based on a pre-sale credit check of their personal credit, you're willing to accept their backup—you're back on the sales track.

3. Include, as part of your request for any pre-sales credit check, your estimation of the prospect's current and future credit requirements. The more your credit department knows about a prospect's credit needs, the better it can determine if your company can meet them.

Many prospective purchasers view credit limits the same way they view basketball or hockey scores—namely, the higher the better. They don't think of credit limits as objective, reason-or-need based numbers ("because of your corporate character, capacity and capital we'll let you charge up to $5000"). Instead, they think of lines of credit as a buyer vs. supplier scorecard, a kind of corporate competition fought over a few fine points of payment.

As part of their game plan, these prospects typically request pie-in-the-sky credit limits. How many times have you had a buyer request "as much credit you can give me" (translation: more than I deserve) or "at least as much credit as you give my competitor" (translation: base my credit limit on my competitors', rather than my own, track record) or "at least as much credit as I can get from your competitor" (translation: base my credit limit on your competitive fears, not objective facts).

This perspective on credit has one major flaw: it doesn't lead to practical programs. Why? Because it is greed-based, rather than need-based. As a result, it does not reflect your customer's (or your company's) best financial interests. Giving a customer more credit than it needs is counterproductive. You encourage it to buy more product than it can afford (that is, more than it can comfortably pay for). You discourage suppliers in other industries from giving it credit, making it impossible for the customer to fulfill its other material needs.

Giving customers more credit than they need/deserve often creates a lose-lose situation. That's why all of your requests for pre-sale credit checks must be accompanied by a realistic—rather than an idealistic—assessment of the prospect's current and long-term credit needs. You want to facilitate, rather than debilitate, your customer's business. And you want profits, rather than problems, for your own.

Why an Estimation is Necessary

There are at least four reasons that your credit department needs this credit guestimation before making its initial investigation.

First, knowing the amount of credit that a prospect is going to need helps guide the research process, keeping it both cost- and effort-effective. If a prospect will need very little credit, the credit department can put a little less effort into the investigation. Conversely, if the prospect is likely to need a lot of credit, your credit and collections department has a lot of work to do. You can think of it this way: intelligent people put a lot more effort into selecting a house or a spouse than they do in selecting a shirt or a skirt. The higher the risk, the higher the investment, the greater the research.

Your credit department requires this early estimation of the prospect's credit needs so that it can pass the information on to any relevant credit references. When a credit reference knows that you're processing a request for a high credit limit, it is not as likely to offer cursory corporate comments. References know that they can be sued for making a questionable client appear to be risk free. This legal leverage makes honesty more than the best policy. It makes honesty the only safe policy—for the reference company and, of course, for your own.

Having your estimate of a prospect's potential credit needs makes it easier for your credit department to circumvent any potential problems. For example: your prospect, the XYZ Company, wants to purchase $5000 worth of your company's products every month. If you limit XYZ to a $5000 line of credit, it will be forced to pay in full every billing period if it is to continue its credit purchasing. In short, you offer credit terms, but they terminate before any long-term damage can be done.

Your early estimate of a prospect's potential credit needs will make it easier for your credit department to brainstorm potential payment alternatives. Assume the XYZ Company needs a $5000 credit limit but due to its lack of capacity/capital/character does not qualify for our standard credit terms. If your credit department is aware of this credit complication before a sale is actually in the works, it has time to work out a workable "yes, if" solution.

The primary question is how to safely give the XYZ Company a $5000 credit line. Your credit department can probably identify a number of acceptable answers. For example, your company will grant XYZ a $5000 line of credit *if* its corporate officers is willing and able to sign personal guarantees. Your company will grant XYZ a $5000 credit line *if* its parent company or a major buyer are willing to co-sign on the credit line. Your company will grant XYZ a $5000 credit line *if* it is collateralized. Your company will grant XYZ a $5000 credit line *if* doing so is a sound business decision (as discussed in Chapter 1). In short, where there's a will—and time to think about potential "ifs"—there's a way.

Credit limits are an important issue. Offer too low a credit limit to a prospect, and you'll kill the sale. Seek too high a credit limit, and your credit department won't be able to live with the risk. That's why it's up to you to make an initial credit estimate that's realistic, rather than idealistic. Your best guess is the credit department's best place to start.

4. Once your prospect is ready to place its first order, your credit department may come to you for some important credit answers. Consider yourself the credit department's most valuable source of credit information. Be its eyes and ears, a conduit of empirical evidence. What you see and hear may substantiate or negate other less reliable credit information.

Most of the credit information available to your credit department will come via a pile of processed paper. Popular paperwork includes: credit reports from credit reporting companies (such as NACM's National Data Base, Dun & Bradstreet and TRW), written business and credit references from current suppliers or associates, and financial statements (both audited and unaudited) from the prospect itself.

These reports are critical to the credit decision-making process, but they can't stand alone. While they definitely shed some necessary light on a prospect's creditworthiness, they don't hold a candle to the sensitive information that you, the professional salesperson, can illuminate. Written reports are second to an enlightened salesperson's empirical evidence. If this surprises you, it shouldn't. Written credit information has inherent limitations and risks.

Credit reports, credit references and financial statements: the basic problem with these credit resources is their sources. Each of these can be intentionally or accidentally undermined. For example, the accuracy of credit reports cannot always be assured. In fact, credit reporting companies admit upfront that they cannot "guarantee the accuracy, completeness or timeliness of the information provided."

Credit reports may mislead by omission. Credit references (as noted earlier) may not volunteer or pass on negative payment information for fear of legal reprisals. Through this inaction, they force the credit reporting company to accidentally (and unknowingly) accentuate the positive. Thus, a credit report's information could be badly skewed. And skewed information is misconstrued information.

Credit reports may be also be outdated. Some credit reporting companies only update their reports every 120 days or so.[11] By the time a report hits its 110 day mark, the company-in-question's credit position may have changed markedly. Relying too heavily on an out-of-date report may have heavy credit and collection consequences.

Finally, generic credit reports may not have much relevance for firms in a protected sales or payment position. For example, according to the credit reporting companies, in the last six months, XYZ has been delinquent in paying off debts to a print shop, janitorial supplies firm and a bookkeeping service. You'd like to extend credit to XYZ, but you wonder, "Is XYZ's credit history going to repeat itself?"

The answer to this question depends on what you sell. Note that XYZ's delinquent payments all involved generic, easy-to-replace suppliers. If you sell a custom or proprietary product that XYZ needs, it can't afford to procrastinate on your payments. It won't abuse you because it can't afford to lose you.

The answer to this credit question also depends on you. If your credit department insists on signed personal guarantees from XYZ's corporate officers, you can bet that the company will pay on time. The cosignatories will see to it. After all, they don't want the payment to come out of their own pockets. In short, if you have reason to believe that your credit experience with XYZ would differ greatly from that of its other suppliers, you may have reason to grant XYZ credit.[12]

Credit references and financial statements, like credit reports, are both important and impeachable. Relying only on these written resources can cause a credit department to miss the handwriting on the wall. How? Again, consider the sources of these resources.

Most references/financial statements are supplied by credit applicants. As a result, they're prone to be positive. Think about it. You wouldn't hire a job applicant based on a character reference from his

[11] Unless a "new report" is specifically requested.

[12] Of course, this cuts both ways. Your company might have a less secure position than the credit references cited in the credit report.

mother, so why would you extend credit to a prospect based on information from its hand-picked references or financial statements? When a prospect controls an information source, it can control the information your credit department receives.

Your Personal Observations Are Important

Clearly, a credit department can't rely solely on credit reports, credit references or financial statements. It needs information from a source it can trust. It needs information from you.

Your credit department doesn't believe everything it sees on paper, but it does believe what you see in person. When you observe a prospective customer firsthand, you're looking out for the company's best interests. You know what to watch for. You keep your eyes open for signs of financial trouble. And, when you see these signs, you see to it that your credit department is made aware of them.

Most salespeople know the obvious warning signs. Many can be seen at the prospect's place of business. Is morale high or highly overrated? Is the mood one of friction, frustration or friendliness? Are the people all working hard, or hardly working at all? When a company is sinking, company morale usually goes down with the ship.[13]

Note: Pay particular attention to the purchasing personnel. Is the purchasing agent angry, apathetic, cynical, depressed? Are your meetings continually interrupted so that the purchaser can solve problems or crises? Does he continue to "almost" place orders or, having made them, does he quickly cancel them? If the purchasing agent doesn't appear to be doing his or her job, perhaps that's because there's no money with which to do it.

[13] All credit information needs to balanced against the information received from other sources. That's why your information is so important. Some information will be positive, other data will be negative, all of it may be true from the sources' perspectives. It isn't always easy to discern the truth. Consider this quote, reprinted from the July 1988 issue of *Inc.* magazine.

"In our company our middle managers knew almost as much about our problems as the officers...They tended to leave for more secure jobs.

"And because these former middle managers were more willing to talk about the company than were former officers, they provided our customers and vendors with more detailed information about our problems.

"You do have to keep this information in perspective, however. In our case, at least, the information was distorted because the middle managers were better informed about our problems than our solutions. For instance, they saw that we couldn't pay our bills on time, that our inventory was piling up and that our margins were low. But top management hadn't told them about the new loan agreements and sales contracts we were working on, or about the favorable effect our increasing volume would have on our margins."

Evaluate the prospect's plant. Is it busy? Well supervised? Well staffed? Efficient? Clean? Are many deliveries being made (good)? Are many product returns coming in (bad)?[14] Does the company look like a going concern, or like one that's going down the drain?

Consider any indirect input. Have you heard anything questionable from other salespeople ("I stopped calling on XYZ because...") or your other clients ("They're no competition anymore! Why, I just heard that..."). Have you heard anything interesting from the prospect's clients (e.g., "XYZ is offering us a fantastic fast-pay discount because it needs cash flow badly"). Who makes deliveries to the prospect, and would they be willing to give your credit department a credit reference?

Your prospects undoubtedly get products (and cold calls!) from other credit-minded companies. You'll find hints all over its office in the form of sales premiums.[15] Look for names (potential references!) on: pens, pencils, note pads, calendars, rulers, letter openers, plastic portfolios, binders, coffee mugs, coasters, etc. And don't forget to check out those corporate Christmas cards! Let the credit department know who's calling on your prospect so that they can make a few profitable calls of their own.

Don't get the impression that credit reports, business references and financial statements are useless. They're not. They just shouldn't be used alone. Direct, unbiased information from you is what gives these two-dimensional reports the depth they need.

Your credit department wants to see what you hear (and hear what you see) on your appointed rounds. Make it a point to pass on your impressions, your observations, your knowledge. This will make it easier for the credit department to artfully construct an accurate pre-purchase credit picture.

5. After the initial sale appears imminent, but before it is a done deal, obtain any necessary credit information (credit references and/ or financial statements), or insurance (personal financial guarantees or cosigners) directly from the prospect.

---

[14] Check for boxes noted "scrap," "return to vendor for rework," "not what we ordered," or "delivery refused."

[15] Many sales premiums outlast sales relationships, so they can also help you locate potentially negative credit references.

For a lucky few of your prospects, qualifying for credit is a virtual cakewalk. Their pre-sales credit check will clearly indicate that they can take credit for taking credit seriously. According to their track records, their payments are always made in full and on time. They maintain excellent financial ratios. They have the capital and capacity to handle additional credit. In other words, when these prospects come knocking on your door, your credit department will run to let them in. You probably won't be asked to obtain their credit references, financial statements and/or personal guarantees. Your credit department will already know all it thinks it needs to know.

Credit-Checking Marginal Prospects

Then there's the majority of your customers: the "marginals."[16] Their credit records (if they even exist) either leave a lot to be desired or leave a lot to the imagination. If you want to do business with the marginal masses—and of course you do, they're invariably going to provide the bulk of your business—you'll have to help your credit department obtain the necessary financial information. This may include prospect-supplied credit references, financial statements and personal financial guarantees.

Collecting each category of business information presents its own special challenges, with credit references being the easiest to obtain, and personal guarantees being the most difficult.

Collecting credit references is a piece of cake that needn't upset your peace of mind. Most companies request references as a matter of course, almost as a mere formality. Customers, particularly those with questionable credit (and they know who they are), are used to reference requests. Asking for these won't ruffle any feathers.

Chances are, your credit and collections department will request at least four or five current references. The more the better. Ironically,

[16] What are marginal customers? They have several common characteristics. They are currently, or are likely to become, slow pay accounts. They carry a higher degree of risk. And they are *everywhere*.

It is difficult to avoid marginal customers. Very few companies are able to obtain and maintain solid gold reputations. Most companies contain some degree of tarnish on their payment histories. Some pay late because they like to dam their cash flow. Other companies overbuy and get themselves into trouble. A few have payment problems as a function of their business season. Some lose their excellent track records as they lose their business edge (they are overshadowed by a competitor, top managers move on, their products lose appeal, their geographic area or industry faces tough economic times, etc.). Credit reputations are like ice: a little business heat and they're no longer solid.

Any customer can be, or can become, a marginal one. For the record, marginal customers are your typical customers. That's why a credit department typically puts a great deal of effort into its credit decisions.

your credit colleagues probably won't use these references as actual references. They will most likely be used to track down other, more remote, references—suppliers that, because of past payment problems, may not be sold on (or still selling to) your prospect.

For example: Your prospect, Company A, may give you XYZ Ltd. as a credit reference. Your credit staffers will try to obtain, from XYZ, the name of any company or individual that XYZ received as an initial credit reference. They may be able to acquire the names of Company A's former suppliers, accountant, attorney, bank or loan officer, co-signer, corporate directors, etc. These references may have much to say about A, particularly if they parted ways over the way payments were imparted.

Your credit department may also request references from specific kinds of companies. For example, a credit staffer will want to talk to Prospect P's major suppliers because that will help establish maximum credit guidelines. Major suppliers also tend to know more about a company, and its business prospects, than its minor suppliers do.

A credit staffer will also want to talk to Prospect P's minor suppliers, particularly those who can be replaced easily.[17] If Prospect P treats easy-to-replace references right, it will probably do right by your firm.

Collecting financial information (balance sheets, profit and loss or operating statements, cash flow projections, lists of current guarantees/liens/pledges/leases, etc.) is a little more complicated. Most firms are hesitant to flaunt their financials. Why? Some do a poor job of keeping good records, others do a good job of tracking their poor performance. Many firms are privately afraid their financial information could become public knowledge. No bones about it: Few firms will graciously allow your credit department to look for skeletons in their record-keeping closet.

This desire for privacy can be complicated by another concern: credit department dictates. Your credit cronies are probably going to insist that a prospective customer submit its information on their approved financial forms. This is not done to be high-handed, it is done to prevent the underhanded manipulation of data. For example, assume that Prospect P lists on its balance sheet an accounts receivables total of $50,000.

[17] Examples: Publishers, nonprofessional service firms, generic equipment suppliers, typesetters, office supply firms, janitorial services, photographers, graphic artists, printers, florists, mail order companies, delivery companies, temporary employment firms, landscapers, maintenance services, etc.

While this looks like a firm figure, the firm may be using it to hide a multitude of sins. Like what, you ask? Consider this:

• It's possible that Prospect P has $50,000 in current accounts. It's also conceivable that this $50,000 is 120 days or more past due, and as a result, would be difficult (if not impossible) to collect.

• Prospect P's $50,000 figure may be the sum total it is owed by many booming businesses, but there's also some chance that a majority of this money is owed by a single large, but financially failing, firm.

• Prospect P's $50,000 figure may indicate true financial capacity, or it could be pledged to others as the result of a prior agreement/purchase. Fifty thousand dollars in A/R won't do your company much good if $49,000 is pledged to some other supplier.

• The $50,000 could all be a function of product purchases, or the figure could be dysfunctionally indicative of $5,000 in actual purchases and $45,000 in interest accrued on past due accounts (interest charges that P might be willing to forgive if its debtors are forthcoming with their $5000 in payments). Only P's accounts receivable clerk knows for sure, and you can be sure that he or she isn't going to spill the beans voluntarily.

Clearly, the $50,000 figure in and of itself is a meaningless number. However, if your credit department were to interpret it incorrectly, the credit consequences could be catastrophic. To prevent this possibility, your credit cohorts may have designed financial forms that require a prospect to come clean with its dated dirty laundry ("How much of this is x days old, how much is y days old, how much of this total is interest...). The problem is, cagey customers don't like it when generic forms (and the unvarnished truth) hang them out to dry.

Note: Many credit departments print their required financial forms on self-addressed, stamped mailers (ones that seal at the end to prevent prying) because they insist that information be forwarded via the U.S. mail. This reduces the possibility of fraud, because mailing fraudulent financial information in an attempt to obtain credit is a federal offense. Unfortunately, while this "insurance" makes sense to credit people, it can incense sensitive prospects.

Securing personal financial guarantees and credit cosigners is the most problem-prone process of all. Some prospects will not qualify for credit in the traditional sense. Credit research will indicate they lack the character, capital and/or capacity to manage credit. Since they can't handle standard-issue credit, and your company doesn't want to get handled, the job calls for creative credit criteria.

Your credit department may offer the prospect a "Yes, if" proposition: *Yes,* we will give you a line of credit *if* it is secured by a personal guarantee or credit cosigner. Said guarantees are often provided by business owners, stockholders/investors, top management, parent companies, or venture capitalists (assuming, of course, these individuals/organizations have sufficient character, capacity and capital to cover the credit obligations).

The arrangement makes sense, but it probably won't make friends. When your credit department requests this kind of second-hand security, your prospect will probably consider it a slap in the face. It won't want to admit that the guarantor or cosigner is the one who qualifies for the credit, not the prospect.

Requesting Sensitive Credit Information

Given the potential unpleasantness, it's no surprise that most salespeople would rather be audited by the IRS than request credit information or security from their prospects. "Money doesn't bother me," says one salesperson. "I can deal with product price and value issues, no problem. But it's difficult for me to request financial information from my prospects. I feel as though I'm trying to serve two mutually exclusive masters: sales and credit. How can I convince my customers that I'm looking out for their best purchasing interests when my actions subversively suggest that we won't, for credit purposes, be able to sell them the products they need?"

Fortunately, when it comes to requesting sensitive credit information from prospects, there are a few tricks of the trade. If the pre-sale credit check is somewhat thin (or contains some questionable contradictions) and all the credit department wants is some supportive statistics or additional insight, you will need to:

• Request the necessary information at the proper time. Don't ask for confidential credit information before your prospect is solidly sold on the product. Premature prodding will simply give the prospect another reason to reject your product. Who needs another sales objection?

Ask for confidential information after the prospect is sold on your product but before the sale is actually written up. This ensures that credit issues do not affect product issues ("I'm not going to buy from you because you're more interested in my financial statements than in my purchasing needs") or sales issues ("What do you mean, I can't place that order until you receive credit approval?").

Bonus: To gain additional support for the sale and maintain momentum, you can use the request for confidential information as a closing technique ("Before we write up your order, I'm going to need five credit references and your last six balance sheets").

Timing is everything. You mustn't allow the credit request to complicate or undermine your sales strategy. The two components need to provide mutual support: credit makes the sale possible and without the sale there would be no need for credit. They will peacefully co-exist, if you piece them together properly.

• Project the proper attitude. You and your credit department have a need, a desire and an obligation to ensure that credit is only given where credit is due. You mustn't sell products to prospects who can't or won't pay for them. Remember, you are a salesperson—not a donation distributor. And your buyers should pay only for their own merchandise without having to subsidize the "accidental donations" given to others.

Having the proper attitude means that you make all credit requests firmly, assertively, professionally and calmly. You should never demand sensitive information, simply request it. Your request should, as a matter of course, sound matter of fact. Collecting sensitive information is simply a part of your job, no big deal. Chances are, your prospect has had to provide this type of information before. You weren't the first to request it, and you won't be the last.

Never make legitimate credit requests appear apologetic or uncomfortable. Be businesslike, be direct. Never say, "The credit department insists that I get such and such" or "I'm sorry to bother you but I need..." Apologizing for your actions gives the impression that you are doing something wrong, that the prospect would be within its rights to deny you the data. If you're ever tempted to play apologist ask yourself: "What am I apologizing for? For making sure that my prospects can pay their bills?" Keep in mind that you are giving your prospects a chance to show their creditworthiness. They won't object unless they have something to hide.

Never send the prospect mixed signals. For example: A salesperson tells a prospect that his or her request for critical credit information is a mere formality, a way to appease the credit department. But the prospect knows that no business would invest time, effort and money gathering resources that it doesn't intend to use. This comment, instead of pacifying the prospect, makes the prospect reconsider the salesperson's veracity.

• Stress that your credit request is standard operating procedure, both in your company and in your industry. Prospects don't like to give out sensitive information, but they realize it's a necessary evil. Chances are, they request similar information from their prospective purchasers.[18] *Bottomline:* They don't have to like it; they just have to do it.

What bothers a prospect most is being singled out, having to provide sensitive information when the same is not required of other corporate customers. To counter that argument, you should simply state that all companies whose pre-sale credit checks generate similar information or concerns are required to provide additional credit information.

Remember, your credit department is not interested in discrimination or aggravation. Its focus is strictly on documentation and investigation. When additional credit data is requested, it simply means that the credit department needs more insight before it can approve (think positive!) your prospect's credit request.

• Demonstrate that your request for credit information is, in fact, beneficial to your prospect. Sell your prospect on the idea of providing additional data.

Assume that Firm F's pre-sale credit check came back decidedly dim. Asking it to shed some light on the situation, via additional credit information, works in F's favor. After all, the alternative is a flat-out denial of credit.

Providing additional credit information can help prospects in a variety of ways. It can counteract criticisms created by a misleading credit report. For example, Firm F's credit report may contain erroneous entries. Perhaps a credit crisis belonging to Florida Firm F was accidentally discrediting Iowa Firm F. Maybe a $5000 account listed as past due is actually an account in dispute (an account that would have been paid on time and in full if the prospect's vendor had met its contractual obligations). Perhaps the credit report is 110 days old and a lot has changed in the last 109 days (new sales contracts, an infusion of cash, a

[18] Obtain a copy of the credit application form your prospect gives to its customers. If your prospect requests sensitive information from its applicants, but won't give similar stuff to you, simply ask it to fill out its own form.

new patent, etc.). Insisting that Firm F provide additional credit information would benefit the firm in two ways: (1) it would make Firm F a stronger credit candidate; and (2) it would make Firm F aware that it was being bruised by a misleading credit report.

If Firm F's basic credit information is being incorrectly interpreted by your credit department, additional information can help right the wrong. For example, Firm F has a high accounts receivable balance. That could mean one of two things. One, F has cash flow and/or collection problems (bad). Two, F offers relatively lenient payment terms (net 60 in an industry where net 30 is typical, charges middle-of-the-road interest rates on past due accounts, etc.) which could, in turn, make it easier for F to gain new sales and charge much higher product prices (good). Assuming that Firm F falls under the second category, providing additional financial information will ensure that its savvy sales strategies aren't going to be its credit undoing.

Bottomline: Credit departments only request sensitive information when a credit decision hinges on it. By supplying this information, your prospect is making it possible for the credit department to comply with, rather than deny forthwith, a prospect's request for credit.

• Prove your ability and willingness to handle confidential information in an appropriate manner. Many prospect's secretly fear that their financial faux pas will be discussed indiscreetly over donuts or laughed at over lunch. If you can gain a prospect's trust, you can gain access to its sensitive financial files.

There are a variety of "trust-me" techniques available to salespeople. Your company can post a confidentiality bond, agreeing to forfeit its proceeds should the prospect's financial information be mishandled. Your company can offer to trade credit references or financial statements. Sensitive information can be sent directly to a specific individual within the credit department; secret codes can be used to ensure that only the privileged few know which prospects match which reports.

Finally, you can remind the prospect that your goal is to meet its needs. Because confidentiality is important to it, confidentiality is important to you. Your company would never do anything that would cause the prospect to lose faith in you or cause you to lose its business.

If this latest prospect-provided supporting evidence (credit references and financial statements) indicates the need for more solid support (personal guarantees/cosigners), things can get sticky. That is, unless you stick to the following guidelines:

• Calmly walk the prospect through your firm's personal guarantee form.[19] Cover every relevant who, what, when, where, why and how. Treat the guarantee like a done deal, like something that is done all the time, and you'll have the job done in no time. If you act like getting the signature is a challenge, your prospect will challenge the need to sign it.

• Stress that the personal guarantee is for a limited time only. Once the prospect proves its creditworthiness, the personal guarantee can and will be cancelled. The personal guarantee is a short-term shot in the arm, not a long-term lifeline.

• Indicate that a personal guarantee shouldn't cost the prospect (or its guarantor) any money. Only in the event of a payment problem does the personal guarantee come into play. If the guarantor has faith in the prospect, he should be willing to potentially put his money where his mouth is. If the guarantor won't back up his company, see if you can determine why he's backing off. Perhaps things are even worse than they look.

As a salesperson, you don't need to know everything there is to know about credit references, financial statements or personal guarantees. It's enough to know how to get them from your marginal prospects. It's probably a lot easier than you think. If you can get sales, you can get sensitive information. Done right, it's not even a hard sell.

6. As part of the pre-sale credit check, try to estimate the profit margin your company would receive from each prospect's business. The greater the profit margin your company can make, the greater the risk your company will take.

Making credit and collection decisions is, in large part, a kind of socially acceptable gambling. Since there is no guarantee that a customer will pay its invoices, your credit department can only play the odds and hope that it won't be odd man out when it comes to getting its money!

Fortunately, a historical perspective can successfully stack the debt deck. For example, if a prospect's credit report and credit references

[19] Do not allow the prospect to amend or alter anything on the guarantee form. Even small changes, such as changing the signature line from "John Jones" to "John Jones, president" can reduce your corporate credit coverage. The aforementioned change, for example, would amend the guarantee so that it is corporate, rather than personal, in nature. In essence, John Jones as president would be guaranteeing that his company would guarantee its own credit.

indicate that it has always paid its bills in full and on time, chances are it would handle your invoices with the same solicitude. If past financial records indicate that the prospect tends to have adequate money in the bank, giving credit to it is probably as safe as money in the bank. While there are no sure things, winning track records indicate that a prospect is a relatively safe credit bet.

Still, a good gambler looks at more than just his odds of winning.[20] He also considers the potential payoff. Few gamblers would buy a $1.00 lottery ticket if the total purse prize were $2.00. However, most would gladly spend a buck if they thought they could win back $2 million. At some point, the opportunity to win will overshadow the likelihood of loss.

Before placing any bet, professional gamblers will consider the risk and possible payback. Before making any credit decision—particularly a risky one, one that involves a marginal customer—your credit department will essentially do the same thing. It will try to determine: (a) how much profit the prospect will bring your company, and (b) how likely it is that the firm will pay fast and fully.

Consider the case of the low-margin (low payback) product. Let's say that your company's overall average gross profit margin is 20 percent. Prospects that purchase product lines with a significantly lower than average gross profit margin (15 percent or less) had better come with compensating criteria. These might include an excellent credit record, top references and a long, strong financial performance. Ideally, its business will also offer indirect economic enhancements. If you help this company with credit, will it help your company build distribution in a previously under-serviced geographic or market area, reduce shipping expenses and inefficiencies, maximize your manufacturing capacity/opportunities, increase product desirability/recognition, or smooth seasonal sales slumps? In short, is there something special about this prospect's business that will make up for the 7 percent shortfall?

Why the more-than-marginal concern? Because there is no margin, no cushion, to cover administration or collection costs. There is no margin to cover the cost of money. There is no margin to cover uncollectible accounts. In short, there is no margin for credit-granting errors. A credit

[20] The amount of "looking" that a credit department does before taking a credit gamble is directly linked to the amount of credit requested by the prospect. A $50,000 line of credit deserves more scrutiny than a $500 line segment.

department soon discovers that it takes a lot of paying customers to make up for every dollar of past due debt. That's particularly true when what is being sold is low-margin material.

Now assume that the product line being purchased has a 30 percent gross profit margin (vs. the 20 percent corporate average). Here the credit department has room to maneuver. Because of the potential payback, it can afford to offer credit to the less lucrative, cash-crunched corporation. It can consider doing business with businesses that aren't doing so well. Why? Because high-margin products/accounts can withstand a higher margin of credit-granting error. Here it takes only a few will-pay winners to cover a credit-caused catastrophe.[21]

Clearly, a product's profit-margin picture can have a staggering effect on a prospect's probability of securing the credit to purchase it. For example, if Company B, a high credit risk, wants to buy item Y, a 10 percent gross profit product, your credit department will probably insist that the transaction be done with cash. Why go out a limb for low-margin marginal customers? The potential payback isn't there.

Why give Company B the credit to purchase a 10 percent gross profit product when there's a 20 percent chance that B will not pay its invoice in full? Why sell the product on credit to Company B if your credit department is going to have to spend double your profit margin to collect the account? Low profit sales should, by definition, be low risk sales.[22]

Conversely, if Company B, a high credit risk, wants to buy item X, a 35 percent gross profit margin product, the risk rules are less strict. Credit and collection departments are willing to accept higher risks when they're coupled with impressive profits. Certainly, your credit comrades will try to find a creative "yes, if" solution, given the potential payback.

It isn't easy to weigh heavy credit decisions. Your credit department must balance a prospect's potential profit payback (and any compensating criteria) against the inherent credit risks and the possible collection costs (which include the seller's cost of money, opportunity costs, collection agency and/or legal fees, administrative costs, etc.).

Direct profit margins aren't the begin all and end all of credit department decisions. In the end, you'll find they are only the beginning.

---

[21] Despite high profit margins, no credit department will offer credit to a customer that it thinks will not pay. Rather, it could choose to offer credit to a customer that it thinks *may* not pay. There's a big difference between the two standards.

[22] The only definitive exception would be if your company needed B's business for reasons other than direct profit (e.g., distribution, product awareness, etc.).

Still, your credit department can't weigh their importance unless you go out of your way to include them in your request for a pre-sale credit check. Your level-headed estimate of each prospect's potential profitability will ensure that all credit judgments are made on a level plane.

7. Tackle your company's terms of sale: define and explain them before there is a credit line, before there is a sale, and consequentially, before there is a problem. A problem defined is a problem confined.

Once you have your foot in the door and a sale in the works, you have to deal definitively with the "in" crowd: the "incorrigibles," the "in-the-darks," the "in-the-computers," and the ever-present "in troubles." Whenever you provide products or services on credit, you have to work with these four categories of customers. You might say the "in" crowd is inherent.

The Incorrigible Customer

Each category carries its own characteristics. The "incorrigibles" have a tendency to procrastinate. No matter what your net payment terms are, you won't net any payment from them until well past the due date.

Some incorrigibles are under the impression that one needn't pay one's bill before receiving a collection letter (or two) from the creditor. Having received a "late again" letter, they will schedule your invoice for payment—but they'll push it back another week, just to pull your chain, just to see if they can pull it off. To them, invoice avoidance is a childish game.

Incorrigibles are usually more interested in controlling the buyer/seller relationship than they are in controlling their cash flow. They'll tenaciously try to take undeserved discounts, make piddling partial payments, insist that the "check is in the mail," and ignore interest-only invoices. They'll act as though you make your rules just so they can break your rules. To credit and collection professionals, and the salespeople they service, an incorrigible customer is a perpetual, profit-draining annoyance.

The In-the-Dark Customer

"In-the-dark" customers characteristically present a more pliable, less provoking, problem. They aren't trying to get away with anything. They're just trying to get a handle on how your invoices work. They're no problem once they're in the know.

Believe it or not, credit terms can confuse even the canniest clerks. Let's say, for example, that your payment terms are net 30. Customer Q's ac-counts payable clerk may not understand the date-related reference.[23] He could be asking himself if net 30 means that:

• the payment is due 30 days after the order is placed

• the check must be received at the supplier's office no later than 30 days after the shipment (invoice) date

• the due date is 30 days after the merchandise arrives

• the check must arrive within 30 days of invoice receipt

The A/P person may also confuse payment dates with mailing dates. His question: Does net 30 mean that the check must be mailed 30 days after the order? Or 30 days after the shipment/invoice date? Or, 30 days after the arrival of the merchandise/invoice?

The A/P person could conceivably confuse working days with calendar days. He wonders: Does 30 days refer to 30 working days? If so, does that mean 30 working days after the order is placed, after the invoice date, or after the merchandise arrives?

This is all fodder for clerk confusion, particularly if the A/P person is new to the industry. Obviously, terms like net 30 may not be as clear as they first appear.

Unfortunately, net due terms aren't the only credit criteria that can catch customers up. Fast-pay discounts also snare their share. Assume your payment terms are 2/10 net 30 (i.e., your company offers a 2 percent discount if an invoice is paid in full within ten days, otherwise the payment is due in full within 30 days). To paraphrase an old cliche, ask six customers what your terms mean and you'll get seven different answers. For example:

• Customer A will argue that in order to deduct the discount, its payment must be made within 10 days of the invoice date.

[23] In many cases, ignorance is understandable. Some of their suppliers probably allow them to use the most liberal interpretation of credit terms. These suppliers simply go along to get along. As long as they know they're going to get paid, they don't get too excited.

• Customer B will believe that to take the 2 percent off the top, its payment must be received within 10 days of the invoice date.

• Customer C will claim that to get the discount deal its check must be dated within 10 days of the invoice date (of course, C may not actually mail the check for two more weeks).

• Customer D will declare that its discount-delivering envelope needs to be postmarked prior to the 10-day deadline.

• Customer E will indicate that its discount-delivering envelope needs to be postmarked early enough that E could expect its payment to be delivered prior to the 10-day timeline.

• Customer F will tell you that it takes the 2 percent discount without respect to the corporation's calendar conditions. It will argue that fast-pay discounts are really trade discounts (see "incorrigibles," page 39). E's accounts payable clerk knows that this argument can be shot down, but he'll try it anyway. You can't blame a guy for trying, even if all he's trying is your patience.

• Customers A, B, C, D, E and F will each decide on a discount definition that suits their individual needs, if not the supplier's.

When dealing with true "in-the-darks," it's important to remember that their ignorance is only a state of mind. When you state, define and explain your credit terms, "in-the-darks" will generally get in line.[24]

It's in the Computer

"In-the-computer" customers would be willing to get in line, but the problem is, they are already on-line. That is, in the computer sense. This gives them an easy "can't pay today" out.

Computerized payables can put your credit and collection department between a rock and a hardware place. Computers make payables easier on buyers but are often tougher on sellers. That's because most computers treat all invoices equally, regardless of their specific timing terms.[25]

[24] Beware of "incorrigibles" masquerading as "in-the-darks." "Incorrigibles" will hide behind any excuse that allows them to stay behind in their payments. Ignorance is blissfully easy to fake.

[25] Computers aren't inherently restrictive. However, many customers claim that they can't do anything about their computer programs, an excuse which is generally accepted.

Consider computers that handle invoices on a 10th prox (or 1-10 EOM) basis. When programs pay this way, it means that all invoices received between the first and last days of a given month will be paid on the 10th of the following month. For example, billings rendered between March 1 and March 31 would be paid by the computer on April 10.

Again, assume your standard credit terms are 2/10 net 30. If you invoice a product to Buyer B on March 1, no amount of prodding will prompt a payment prior to April 10. In short, B has extracted an additional ten days net (from 30 to 40 days) from your company, courtesy of its computer.[26]

If Buyer B makes its payments bi-monthly (a common arrangement is to cut checks on the 10th and the 25th), they've cut your credit conditions some significant slack. On a 10th/25th system, invoices billed between the 1st and 15th of the month would be payable on the 25th of the same month. Billings from the 16th through the end of the month would be payable on the 10th of the following month.

By paying its bills twice (rather than once) a month, Buyer B more than doubles its chances of beating your currently-due deadlines. Unfortunately, disagreements over fast-pay discounts are a common occurrence under the bi-monthly pay plan. Computer-aided customers commonly claim that since they pay their invoices as quickly as they can, they can take the supplier's fast-pay discount. Regardless of any specific-day deadline.[27]

The In-Trouble Customer

The "in-trouble" characters are an entirely different matter—a mostly *money* matter. The "incorrigibles" don't pay on time because they don't want to. The "in-the-darks" don't pay on time because they don't know what they're doing. The "in-the-computers" don't always pay on time because they don't run the payment program, their machine does. Still, all of these troublesome types have a way to pay. They have the means, they have the money.

[26] If possible (and practical), you should try to call on Buyer B toward the end of the month. Hopefully, any invoices can be processed and mailed early enough to make the computer's cut-off date, thus assuring prompt payment.

[27] Explain that fast-pay discounts are not trade discounts. They can be revoked at your company's whim and can only be invoked when a customer meets the credit criteria.

The "in-troubles" are, shall we say, financially indisposed? Their problem is liquidity, not absurdity (incorrigibles), stupidity (in-the-darks), or rigidity (in-the-computers).

The "in-troubles" require careful monitoring. This is particularly true when their troubles are long-term. Perhaps an "in-trouble" is perpetually undercapitalized or overstocked. Perhaps it has a difficult time turning its A/R into Available Resources. Perhaps its pricing strategy has created marginal profits rather than big profit margins. Perhaps its owners/managers tend to take more out of the business than they put in. Perhaps their business plans are riddled with mishaps.

An "in-trouble's" trials are often, fortunately, short-term. Perhaps one of its biggest customers is suddenly slow to pay. Perhaps the company had a miserable month (for example, all of the top salespeople took the same season off). Perhaps a gust of cold weather put a chill on its sales, or perhaps the company was victimized by a robbery, embezzlement, fire, earthquake or hurricane.[28]

Any of these situations will likely generate payment mishaps. When customers have problems, you often end up with problem customers. There's no way around it.

A Six-Point Program for Dealing With Problem Customers

In the greater scheme of things, however, you can come to terms with payment term problems. This six-point program will help you circumvent the situations that all four credit "incurables" have in common. Since you can't determine up front if a prospect will fit into one of these "in" categories, these procedures should be used on all soon-to-be buyers.

• **Discuss/define all payment terms, what they mean, and how they work before the first sale is a done deal.** This way, you can specifically address all of the potential payment problems ("Some people believe that 2/10 net 30 means that payment is due 30 working days after the invoice is received. Of course, what it really means is...").

Note: Because the prospect has yet to place an order or owe on an invoice, it won't be offended by the information. In short, you can preempt potential punches to your profit line without hitting prospects

[28] The interminable trials and tribulations of "in-troubles" will be discussed later relative to special credit terms.

below the belt. What you're practicing is education, not intimidation.

• **After reviewing all of the credit term terminology with the prospect, have him or her initial every related section of your company's credit application form/sales contract.** This will undercut any attempt to use confusion ("We didn't know what that term meant") or ignorance ("Nobody ever told us that") as a debt defense. Most "ins" are more likely to pay if they have no easy out.

• **Emphasize that in signing the credit application contract, the prospect legally commits to paying all invoices in accordance with your credit terms. Adherence to these conditions is required.** That's why they are included in The Contract. When a business breaks a contract, it puts the brakes on building a good business reputation.

• **Stress that when conditions of the credit contract (payment terms) are violated, your company may be forced to forward that fact to certain credit bureaus (perhaps "on the advice of legal counsel").** Disclosing information about delinquent debtors is often a membership requirement of local credit co-ops.

• **Communicate the benefits of prompt payments.** Forwarding finances fast will promote a good corporate image, a sound credit record, and a trusting buyer/supplier relationship. Prompt payments will also allow a company to take advantage of fast-pay discounts, which engender more quantitative qualities. They immediately add more black to any business' bottom line.

For example, would your buyers like to make 36 percent on their money, risk free? Wouldn't everybody? Well, this offer is a "limited time" offer and it's only available to quick-paying purchasers.

Explanation: This offer is limited to the ten-day time span referenced in the discount terms 2/10 net net. If your credit terms are 2/10 net 30, the effective interest rate (the customer's prompt purchase payback) is 36 percent.

Exactly what does that mean? Let's say Buyer B has an invoice of $1000 which it pays in full within ten days. Buyer B pays $980, deducting the discount of 2 percent or $20. By paying in 10 days rather than 30, it essentially loses the use of the $980 for twenty days. If B had invested this $1000 for that twenty days and earned $20 in interest, B would have earned 36 percent per annum interest on its principle.

Bottomline: If B can get a bank loan at less than 36 percent annual interest, it would be money ahead to borrow from the bank so that it can pay your invoices early. If B's other invoices carry a lower effective interest rate (or offer no fast-pay discount at all), B would be money ahead to pay your bills first. In fact, it might be money ahead to pay your invoices quickly, even if it means postponing and paying interest on its other bills. Thanks to your fast-pay discount, your credit department will be ahead and shoulders above the rest!

Effective interest rates are an excellent discount-selling tool. Popular discount/credit terms include:

Discount	Discount Timeline	Net Due Date	Effective Interest Rate
1/2	10 days	30 days	9 percent
1	10 days	30 days	18 percent
2	10 days	30 days	36 percent
2	10 days	60 days	14 percent
2	30 days	60 days	24 percent
2	40 days	60 days	36 percent
3	10 days	4 months	10 percent
3	30 days	60 days	36 percent
3	10 days	30 days	54 percent
4	10 days	4 months	13 percent
4	10 days	60 days	29 percent

• **Show the consequences of payment procrastination.** Poor credit records, poor supplier relationships, poor corporate image, etc., all are part of the payment procrastination downpour. Slow-pay purchasers have to prepare themselves for a storm of costly criticism.

And that's just part of the problem. Slow payments can also force buyers to part with more of their money. Interest charges (particularly minimum interest charges of say, $10 or $20 per month) can run up bills faster than a cashier on commission. Finance charges of 18 percent and 22 percent aren't uncommon (although they pale in significance next to the effective interest rates on common fast-pay discounts). Buyers who can't afford to add 18 percent per annum to the cost of their products will find slow-pay programs a very bad buy.

Remember, as tough as these subjects are to discuss, you're having this discussion before the prospect has had any problems. Since you're not pointing any fingers, prospects won't take it personally when you point out the facts.

If you're in the sales profession you're going to have trouble with the "in" crowd. They're like the common cold: everybody gets them, and nobody knows how to completely avoid them.

Fortunately, a strong dose of Vitamin C (that's "C" for communication) will do the same thing for your buyer/supplier relationship that it did for your credit/sales relationship. It will take problems that are a real bear, and make them almost bearable.

Fast-pay discounts of 2/10 net 30 cannot (*must not*) be deducted beyond the designated 10-day date. If they are taken, they must be given back (usually via an addition to the next invoice). Tell your customers that bottomline discounts only go to those customers who follow the rules. Allowing unqualified customers to take discounts is discriminatory (perhaps even illegal). At the very least, they are unfair—to you, your company and your other clients.

8. Make sure that requests to your sales manager and credit department for "special credit terms" are few and far between. They should only be considered when the prospect is a VIP (Valuable Individual to Profits).

Special Credit Terms

There are two categories of "special credit terms." One is legit; the other, not a bit.

On the pseudo side, you have what could facetiously be called "customer granted special credit terms." In an ideal world, your company would set its credit criteria (say, 2/10 net 30) and all of your customers would abide by them. Unfortunately, in the real world, customers often ignore their supplier's dollars and cents dictates. They effectively make their own rules by choosing to ignore yours ("Let's see, this says 2/10 net 30, so we'll pay this in two months and see if we can still take the discount"). They don't make the rules, but via their payment behavior, they still rule the roost.

It's sad but true. Even if your company doesn't grant liberties to its credit customers, some businesses are going to take them. They figure that since the customer is always right, the customer has a right to set its own payment terms. Doubtless you've heard some variations on these familiar financial themes: "We'll pay you...when we have the money...or just as soon as our bookkeeper comes back from the Bahamas...or the minute so-and-so pays his bill." Translated what this really means is, "We'll pay you when we absolutely have to—and by the way, you'd better not have charged us interest!"

Real honest-to-goodness special credit terms originate from the sales side. The buyer doesn't summarily take advantage of its supplier. Instead, the supplier gives the buyer the advantage. This different perspective is what makes special credit terms a horse of a different color. Unfortunately, this is one "gift horse" that every salesperson should look squarely in the mouth. Why? Because, as you'll soon learn, special rules have teeth; and they can take a big bottomline bite out of even the most well-meaning manufacturer.

Standards for Special Credit Terms

In order to work, special credit terms must meet the following standards:

• **Special credit terms must not be a Standard Operating Procedure.** They are an exception to the rule, an exceptional measure that is taken when a prospect can't abide by the company's current credit rules. They are not, cannot, must not be offered to everyone (if they were, they wouldn't be special!). They are not, cannot, must not be offered unless they fulfill a dire buyer need and a higher supplier creed. For example, special credit limits will only be extended when the company can expect a gross average profit on the prospect's transactions of 25 percent or more.

• **True special credit terms are offered *for just cause*, not *just because*.**[29] If, for example, a prospect is engaged in a highly seasonal business (for example, it sells toys, power mowers or snow skis) or had an unusually bad season (due to a fire, flood, death of an owner, new location, heavy losses due to a non-recurring expense, etc.) it may need a credit break to help it break even. Special terms are probably justified

[29] True special credit terms are a privilege—not a right—and they need to be earned. Either the buyer earns them via its past track record, current behavior, or short-term need, or the buyer deserves them because of its strategic importance to the supplier.

in these instances. However, "just because the prospect asked" is not just cause. It's just plain counterproductive.

• **True special credit terms are only offered when a company has something to gain from a cash-poor prospect—that is, when the transaction makes business, if not credit, sense.** The seller may have the broad aim of "increased sales," or it could have a more defined target in mind (market penetration in Territory Y, better utilization of manufacturing capacity in the third quarter, head-to-head competition with Competitor Z in its traditional sales stronghold, etc.). No pain (as in suffering the low-profit margins of special credit terms), no gain. A company that keeps its eye on the prize may see special credit terms as a winning ticket.

• **True special credit terms are always offered for *a limited time only.*** Companies that provide long lasting credit deals soon find that they are doing more than giving their customers a break. They are breaking themselves financially. It's fine to provide short-term fiscal support; it's fatal to become a long-term credit crutch. If your standard credit terms are realistic, reasonable and responsible, your prospects should have no trouble meeting your high standards.

• **True special credit terms always require the approval of both the sales manager and the credit and collections department.** Together, they generate the balanced perspective (business vs. budget) that is necessary to make the right credit decision. While it's tempting, as a salesperson, to ramrod special terms through the home office, to do so would be an act of rampant irresponsibility. It could also have serious ramifications. The financial fallout inherent in special credit terms needs to be considered by those—or on behalf of those—who are most likely to be affected.

• **True special credit terms carry a high cost to your company, and not just in direct monetary terms.** There's the inherent cost of conflict. Let's say you have two customers, Buyer B and Purchaser P. While B is offered special credit terms, P is considered "nothing special."

When Purchaser P discovers it's being offered second-class credit terms, it's likely to take its business elsewhere—to one of your competitors who will treat it like a class act. In short, special credit terms may have helped you buy B's business, but in return they cost you P's purchases. You traded P, a purchaser who could pay the bills, for a customer who can't (at least, not without help).

Another special credit conflict is bound to arise between salespeople. Put yourself, figuratively, in P's position. How would you feel if you discovered that your customers had to meet all of the company's standard credit terms, while customers serviced by other salespeople were being met halfway? It doesn't seem fair (that's because it isn't). You'd probably feel that the company had sold you and your customers out. And at a discount, no less! That kind of attitude wouldn't help your morale or your money-making.

Special credit terms can also generate especially ugly competitive chaos. Credit term wars are to price wars what world wars are to squirt-gun fights. Price wars are controllable, in that they deal with one issue: margins. Credit terms are not so convincingly confined. If competitors bait their buyers with longer nets, bigger discounts, interest free "loans," or larger credit limits, your company may be on the hook as well.

You'll have to offer the same (or better) credit terms to keep your customers. And as the credit terms expand exponentially, your company's (and your competitors') profit margins are going to contract contrarily. The only winners will be your can-due, purchase-without-paying customers. They will, unfortunately, begin to see these comely special terms as their due and fight to keep them coming.

Conflict considerations aside, special credit terms are a very pricey proposition. Consider just one variation: the long net due date. Extending one's net numbers will affect a wide range of corporate components. It would have a negative influence on:

• Cash flow projections. If your company expects to collect its invoices in 15 days and that number suddenly jumps to 30, you've got double trouble in the dollar department. The company no longer has cash flow, it has a cash drip.

What's worse, out of this financial drop in the bucket your company needs to wring out enough cash to cover its outflow obligations: paychecks, taxes, rent, utilities, materials expenses, advertising, loan/equipment payments, etc. Long net terms can make it difficult to meet these short-term payment obligations.

In short, special credit terms can financially affect more than just your buyers. Because they limit your corporate liquidity, they can also impact your relationship with suppliers.

• Bad debt exposure. As noted earlier, the older a debt is, the more difficult (and more expensive) it is to collect. Essentially, you end up trading the "benefits" of offering special credit for the "fits" customers throw when they are the recipients of collection calls, dunning letters, collection agency actions or lawsuits.

There will be increased collection costs, including long distance telephone calls, mailing registered/overnight mail, telegrams, collection agency fees, legal expenses and/or administrative overhead. Companies which often offer special credit terms may need additional collection experts.

Increased bad debt exposure is a problem on two levels. As noted above, it aggravates the aggregate totals and it unjustifiably indemnifies individual customers.

First, consider the larger picture. Statistical reporting of the nature and condition of a company's aggregate receivables has recently become much more sophisticated. Thanks to computer chips, a company can tell much faster when its fiscal chips are down. Finance vice presidents and treasurers are no longer happy with basic A/R information; now they are able to obtain a broader base of data,[30] one that gives them a bird's eye view of any credit terms that might be fouling the financial nest.

The following DSO/special terms exposure comparison chart documents a common correlation. It demonstrates clearly how special credit terms can muddy a profit picture.

DSO/Special Terms Exposure Comparison

	Days Sales Outstanding	Special Terms Exposure (% of debt subject to payment under special terms)
June 30	34 days	6 percent
July 31	39 days	8 percent
August 31	41 days	10 percent
September 30	44 days	14 percent
October 31	46 days	17 percent
November 30	50 days	20 percent

[30] Thanks to sophisticated computer programs, most companies are able to track the following on a monthly or biweekly basis:

1. The total number of days sales outstanding (DSO) in receivables by division, geographical area, product or salesperson
2. The percentage of receivables tied up in standard credit terms and special terms (some even maintain separate reports for particular term deviations)
3. The degree of correlation between these two factors and
4. The evidence of any trend

The problem of debt exposure looks even more serious from a particular purchaser's perspective. Take Company C, for example. It is receiving special credit terms (net 120 days as opposed to the standard net 30 days) from your company because it can't pay promptly. *Note:* Because it can't pay promptly (the way your other customers do!) it is, inherently, a greater risk.

So what happens to Company C, this greater risk? It's able to accumulate even greater debts! Here's the pattern: If Company C purchases $10,000 in product per month, under the 30 day net terms, it would not owe your company over $10,000. Or if it did, the credit department would take immediate action.

Conversely, if Company C purchases $10,000 in product per month and is granted special terms of 120 days net, it could owe your company as much as $40,000 without generating any special attention from the credit department. While any business is risky, this is clearly a very risky business.

• The value of your accounts receivable. As noted earlier, the older the account, the lower its cash value. To paraphrase an old cliche, a buck in the hand is worth two on the books.

There are a number of receivables ramifications your company may suffer when its DSO begins to grow. They can have an immobilizing impact on your company's credit condition. For example, it's likely that your company's bank loan requires it to maintain certain financial ratios. Common control ratios are a debtor's receivables turnover (net sales divided by average receivables), current ratio (current assets divided by current liabilities), and its quick ratio (cash, marketable securities and accounts receivable divided by current liabilities). These ratios are badly battered when a company's credit terms are a deterrent to current payments.

If these financial ratios fluctuate too far from the norm, your firm would normally find itself facing a credit cutoff or, at the very least, paying higher interest on its loan. Both alternatives pack a punitive profit punch.

• Sales. Special credit terms require your credit and collections department to become a credit and *collections* department. Because they increase your risk (more money is outstanding for more time to more risky clients), your credit department will need to practice more diligence.

The more time your credit department has to spend on collections (dealing with current problems), the less time it has to spend on credit (generating new or increased business). The money spent to carry these greater risks can't be used to carry on more positive sales-oriented strategies, such as developing new advertising/marketing plans, increasing travel expenses, adding sales training or providing additional sales support.

Would you rather see corporate resources used to chase after new accounts or chase down old ones?

Ironically, special credit terms cost a company in terms of conflict and money and often buy very little in return. Special term customers are much like price-only customers. They are loyal only to the current deal, and as a result are not very profitable to deal with. They play tug of war with both ends of the rope: if you offer them 30 (rather than 15) days net, they'll take your offer to a competitor and see if it will meet/beat it. If your competitor ups the ante to 45 days, they'll precede any purchase order with a call to you, asking for 60. And so on.

Special credit terms don't buy customer loyalty and they bear a heavy cost. So before your company offers any unusual credit concessions, make sure they meet the following criteria:

• All special terms should be formally and specifically requested by the prospect/customer ("I need terms of net 120 if I'm going to purchase from you"). If you offer special credit terms before they're requested, you're off on the wrong track. If a client truly needs them, he or she should be willing to ask for them...and willing to document the need for them as well.

• The need for special terms should be quantitatively verified. Requests for unique credit conditions can come in two unpalatable flavors: soured financials and bittersweet competitors.

We'll start with the first scenario. Assume that a prospect asks you for special credit terms because it cannot pay its invoices within your typical timeline. The request must be accompanied by objective data which demonstrate the payment problem.

In order to make a case as a charity case, your prospect can present one of two situations. First, it can document (through the use of balance sheets, operating statements, accounts aging reports) that its problem is basically that of adverse cash flow fluctuations. In other words, they can pay, but not today.

The second classic case would be that of the extenuating circumstance. A prospect may be the victim of a flood, fire, earthquake, hurricane, robbery, embezzlement, sudden (and unanticipated) stoppage of a bank loan or venture capital, the death of a principal, a major reshuffling of its top management, a never-to-be-repeated financial faux pas, etc. In the case of both financial problems and extenuating circumstances, the hat-in-hand prospect must make its request with documentation in hand. If it wants you to go the extra mile, it needs to meet you halfway. With documentation of its special credit needs.

Unacceptable documentation would be year-old letters from Suppliers X, Y and Z stating that they "are aware of Buyer B's current financial difficulties and will try to work with it."

The bittersweet competition case is slightly different. In this instance, your buyer is trying to use competitive pressures to manipulate you into giving it a sweet deal. Its case is more likely to be based on greed than need. That's why competitive pressure requires a strong counter measure.

For example, Buyer B tells you that all of your competitors are giving it an extra 90 days net. Are you cowed? Don't be. B is probably feeding you a line of bull. After all, it's probably used this technique many times in the past to get the competitive credit ball rolling.

B's game plan is simplicity itself: B tells Seller S that its competitors are offering terms of net 90. Not to be outdone (just outwitted), Seller S offers Buyer B 90 days net. Buyer B then approaches Sellers T, U and V and insists on the same credit terms that Seller S "offered." Soon, all the sellers have sold out on the issue and Buyer B has bought more time.

The best defense for this offensive technique is the direct approach. Respond to the competitive credit challenge with unruffled reasonableness. Ask Buyer B for copies of its invoices showing the special consideration, or ask for letters or credit applications from the referenced suppliers which both offer and identify the special credit conditions.

Tell the customer that "our company will meet any reasonable competitive situation with respect to prices or terms. All that we require, as a matter of policy, is some evidence of the situation that we must match. Would you please provide us with current documentation?"[31] Check and mate.

Bottomline: If you offer a customer special payment terms, make sure the terms were offered because of money matters, not mind-game manipulation. Because special credit offers should be few and far between, they should only go to those few companies whose orders would otherwise fall between the cracks.

• Stress that all special credit terms are temporary. Unusual credit terms are a function of unusual, short term circumstances. When those unusual circumstances change,[32] the accompanying credit conditions must change with it. Should an exceptional circumstance become the rule (such as the buyer's cash flow fails to improve), you must take exception to the situation and rule out any further special credit. You must insist that your buyer conform to standard credit practice. Otherwise, the special credit terms you offered as a temporary helping hand will quickly get out of hand.

When you communicate any special credit terms to a buyer, you need to use a "yes, but" two-prong approach. First you impress with the "yes": "Yes, this buyer has been given net 120 day credit terms..." Then you stress the rest: "...but this policy applies only to this order," or "but these arrangements will expire within three months," or "but we will review the whole agreement again in 60 days." In other words, when communicating special credit terms, you have to make the right plug: Buyer B is getting an excellent deal now but in *x* days you're going to pull the plug. This is a limited time offer.

You have to be firm when it comes to offering firms special credit terms. Credit concessions are a privilege, something that a buyer has to earn. They are not a right.

Special credit terms are something that a supplier only gives when it's given a good reason. They are a dynamite sales tool, but they can blow up in your face.

9. Acknowledge (and accept) the fact that what your credit department knows about some prospects will indicate that they do not deserve credit. And, yes, your competitors (who may be in the dark datawise) may not see these prospects in the same limiting light.

---

[31] Acceptable documentation would be letters dated last week from Suppliers A and B stating that they will "extend to Buyer B the special credit terms of 2/10 net 90 for the next three months, at which time the need for special credit terms will be reevaluated."

Unacceptable documentation would be year-old letters from Suppliers X, Y and Z stating that they "are aware of Buyers B's current financial difficulties and will try to work with it."

[32] Achange that could be a function of either the buyer (such as if its financial conditions improve) or the supplier (its business goals shift).

There's an old axiom in the credit and collections business: (1) the credit department *always* makes its credit decisions based on a prospect's potential and probable profitability; and (2) in the event that the credit department doesn't *appear* to make its credit decisions based on these two criteria, see (1).

Appearances, like some sales objectives, can be deceiving. You may have a prospect who appears to be minting money, when what it's really doing is passing bad paper. You might see a business that ships products like crazy, but if you looked behind the scenes you'd see that its products are often returned because they aren't shipshape. You'll continuously find companies that spend more time cultivating an image of success than they spend cultivating success itself.

In short, you can't judge a company's books by its camouflaged cover. The successful image you saw at first glance may be a mirage that disappears once you see more objective credit data.

It's possible (even probable) that some of your prospects have had their credit applications summarily rejected (this despite the fact that your credit department's pre-sales credit check—you did request one, didn't you?—came up clean). It can happen. Credit conditions change quickly; furthermore, some companies can covertly shield negative credit information from all but the most determined credit scan. Since few suppliers invest a great deal of time and money on the pre-check, these companies are not usually identified until the first sale is made.

No doubt you're unhappy about the negative news. You have time, effort, money and hopes invested in the sub-par prospect. The prospect isn't very happy about the situation either. It, too, has an invested interest of time, effort and hopes. At times like these, the buyer/supplier relationship can become strained.

Believe it or not, your credit department is as unhappy about this turn of events as you are. Credit departments see themselves as a support service, and having to withhold support is frustrating. The credit staff doesn't like to deal with unhappy (not to mention frustrated, angry, concerned and occasionally abusive) salespeople. It has also invested a great deal of time, effort and money in this prospect. In short, having to turn down a credit application turns everyone off.

Still, there are times when it has to be done. Credit may be the ultimate customer support service, but it's only the end result of an extended and extensive support system. In order to support the customer with a credit line, the credit department has to have evidence to support its decision and the buyer has to have the financial support system necessary to service the debt. If there's no support, the credit application comes up short.

On the surface, a company may look like a good credit risk, but scratch the surface and it may hemorrhage red ink. That's why it's important that salespeople ultimately accept the informed credit judgments of their credit staff. Your credit department has all the necessary credit information at its fingertips, and can put its finger on problems you wouldn't have a chance to see.

For example, Buyer B currently purchases all of its widgets from Supplier X. X has apparently granted B an extensive line of credit with all the trimmings (cash discounts, no-interest invoices, long net due dates). You'd like a piece of the action, but your credit department goes to pieces when you suggest meeting X's credit terms. In fact, your credit department refuses to extend B any credit at all. B's business would have to be C.O.D.—Cash Or Diddly.

Question: Why does X supply B with products on credit when your company will only supply B with products on a cash basis? There are a number of possible explanations. The first is that the X credit factor is only an illusion. Perhaps B is not really getting credit from X. It may make that claim hoping your company will get the message and decide to compete credit-wise.

It's possible that your credit department knows more about B's current creditworthiness than X does. Companies often forget the necessity of monitoring their current customers. Your credit department may be basing its decision on current and complete credit information; X's decision may be off base due to out-of-date data. In short, your credit department may be making the right decision and X may not be making a decision at all, extending credit to B simply by force of habit.

It's possible that the relationship between B and X is a shotgun wedding and X is no longer able to call the credit shots. X may be locked into a virtual or actual insolvency situation with B and have no way out (other than to continue providing credit so that B can hopefully dig its way out of the financial hole). X may have other tight ties to B, ties that bind even when B is at the end of its financial rope. X may have a hidden partnership in (or mutual contract with) B, X may be a co-signatory on one of B's loans, one of B's principals may be on X's Board of Directors, etc. X may be offering B credit the same way you offer your tax payments to the government: realistically but reluctantly.

X may be offering credit to B not because B deserves credit, but because X badly needs sales. For example, X may need to increase sales in an attempt to secure a bank loan, obtain venture capital funding, receive credit from its own suppliers, make itself more attractive to a possible business buyer, or sweeten an initial public offering of its stock. X may be suffering from excess inventory or manufacturing capacity. In short, the credit decision is predicated by X's motives, rather than indicated by B's financials.

Your company may refuse credit to B for external reasons (B doesn't deserve it) or internal ones (we can't grant it). It's possible that your company is in the middle of a cash crunch and can't afford to carry more accounts. Perhaps there was a directive from your reigning top managers, asking the credit department to tighten its credit reins. Maybe extrapolated formulas suggested that liberal credit decisions were generating a negative trend that had to end. Maybe your company is currently manufacturing to the max and can't handle more business. In other words, the credit decision may be a function of your company's internal situation, not B's configuration.

Finally, it's possible that both companies' credit departments saw the same data and simply interpreted it differently. That happens, too. Credit decisions are, in the end, value judgments and people value things differently.[33]

If you're concerned about a credit rejection, you have every right to ask your credit department to justify it. However, you must remember that your credit staff has the final responsibility (and accountability) for credit decisions. It has to be that way. Credit staffs have a difficult job: accelerating sales growth without facilitating bad debts.

It's a sad fact of life that some of your sales prospects are not going to be creditworthy. It's an even sadder fact that when credit-worthless prospects get their applications through, they can throw overall

[33] If you think overly negative credit vaulations are a problem in your company, try the following:

• Keep track of how many prospects your credit department rejects and accepts. How do the two numbers compare? What percentage of your prospects are rejected? Does the amount seem unusually large?

• Keep track of those companies that receive credit from you yet are rejected by your competiors. You'll see that the sword cuts both ways.

• Review all rejected credit applications six months and then twelve months later. Does it appear that your credit department made the right decsions? Is this typical?

corporate profitability for a loop. It's the credit staff's job to only give credit where credit is due. Give them credit for doing the best job they can, even when you resent the results.

Be fair in your analysis. Remember, looking back at the situation is easier than looking forward into it. Hindsight is always 20/20.

10. Remember that no prospects, even those that are fiscally defunct, will be turned away if they are willing (and able) to pay cash for their purchases. Since most credit-poor prospects are already limited to cash and carry payment programs (your competitors won't give them credit either), your cash-only conditions won't surprise them. Furthermore, if you give these prospects a face-saving out, they will go out of their way to give you their business, now and in their more financially-sound future.

These are the best of times (you're about to close a sale), these are worst of times (you need cash from the customer to close it). These are the sales that try men's souls. Perhaps only Shakespeare could capture the angst.

Consider this first worst case scenario. The customer in question was a prospect who, at first glance, appeared prosperous. Now, at second glance, you're wondering what you saw in it during your preliminary peek. It has more image and mirage than it has equipment, more puffery and plans than it has profits, more vacuous visionaries than it has sales. It talks a good show, but its talk is cheap and no evidence supports it. It is clearly not a candidate for credit.

Then there's the second worst case scenario. You have a prospect whom you can tell at first glance doesn't even deserve that second look, at least not in the credit sense. It has no capital, no capacity/cash flow, no character (unless you count the eccentric entrepreneur who runs it). It has no cash-creating or compensating qualities (such as the exclusive patent on a cure for the common cold). It clearly doesn't have what it takes to take on credit. So why are you letting this prospect take up your time?

Even a prospect with a poor (or non-existent) credit record needs to purchase products. In that respect, it is just like any other customer. So why not take the good customers with the bad—and take them both for all the sales they're worth? A poor prospect's cash is at least as good as a rich customer's credit.

When you deal with not-secure-enough-for-credit customers, you will have to secure cash payments in advance. Surprisingly, asking for money isn't any more difficult than asking for sales. It's all in the technique. Just remember the following:

• Cash-poor prospects probably already pay their other suppliers in advance. If your company requires cash-on-the-spot, you're not putting this prospect on the spot. It's undoubtedly been there for quite some time.

• A prospect usually knows far more about its poor fiscal/credit position than you do. It knows it's in trouble and, furthermore, it knows that you know it's in trouble. That's why it won't be troubled when you ask it for cash in advance (although it will undoubtedly ask for credit—there's no harm in trying!).

• Treat this applicant's request for credit with the same respect you would give your more profitable prospects. Don't be curt, or feelings (and sales revenue) will be hurt. Be as sensitive to the prospect's organizational ego as you are to its sales needs. But *never* promise or imply that it will receive any standard (or special) credit terms.

• When the prospect gives you its first order, give it a chance to save face. Tell it that due to the rush nature of its order your company has been unable to complete the normal credit investigation and, for that reason, you need an advance check to cover this initial purchase. Of course, you continue, your credit department will pursue the credit investigation in the sincere hope that regular terms can be offered on the prospect's future purchases. This way, you can land the sale and let the prospect's ego off the hook.

• When the customer gives you its second order, act as though credit was never an issue. Simply ask it to cut a check for *x* dollars "as it did on its last order." This allows you to reinforce the need for cash payments without really forcing the credit issue. It's a win/win situation; you save the sale using consummate tact, and the customer's ego remains intact.

With a little sales savvy, you can simultaneously save face for the customer and save sales for yourself. As an added bonus, this little dose of sensitivity will go a long way in building big customer loyalty. Today's cash-poor customers often turn into tomorrow's cash galore customers.

As noted at the beginning of this chapter, the professional salesperson has to keep running just to stay even. Account attrition is an inherent profit problem. Some current customers will go out of business, others will decide to go to your competitors. Purchasers will come and go in conjunction with your new product lines, marketing strategies, advertising campaigns and credit restrictions. Accounts can fizzle as a function of numerous external phenomenon (macro/micro economic or geographic "growth-slowth," income or property tax strategies, import/export restrictions, etc.). Some businesses will grow beyond your ability to serve them; others will shrink until their purchases aren't worth the effort. Sometimes new purchasing people, or new purchasing needs/wants/values, can make new orders a virtual impossibility.

The point is, if you're going to maintain—not to mention gain—ground in the sales world, you have to hit the ground running. You have to continually bring in new business. The problem is, carrying any new business on the books—be it a new business or simply a new-to-you business—carries a certain amount of additional risk. Fortunately, handled correctly, new accounts also carry with them the certainty of profits.

If you follow the Ten New-Credit Commandments discussed in this chapter, you can minimize credit risk while maximizing credit sales. Used in conjunction with the three C's of the sales/credit relationship—cooperation, communication and courtesy—they will help you add a fourth C—cash—to the corporate coffers.

Chapter 3

The Established Customer

Gaining a new customer could be compared to gaining a spouse. For example, the pre-commitment process is almost identical. You start with the prospecting period ("Is this someone I want to get involved with?"). Then there's the courtship, where you count the prospective partner's pluses and minuses (although quantitative credit checks are usually reserved for the purely proprietary pair-ups). Finally, someone pops the question and the deal is done. The couple lives happily ever after. 'Til death (or debt) do you part.

Don't you wish! In the real world, constructive coupling (whether it's between a couple of people or a couple of conglomerates) takes work.

As discussed earlier, customer attrition is a constant proposition. Sometimes business losses are a function of non-monetary motivators. Customers change suppliers as a function of their business structure, purchasing needs, personnel preferences, technological turnarounds, lax loyalties, varying values, or via a combination of these components. These changes are clearly man-made.

But other customer losses are strictly money-made and money-motivated. The purchasing partnership is doomed—perhaps from the start—by debt difficulty. For example, your relationship with Buyer B gets started off on the right foot, but it is soon subject to a series of major missteps. Buyer B makes a past due payment. As its next faux pas, it intentionally oversteps its credit limit, then kicks up a fuss when your credit department refuses to accept its oversized order. Tempers flare and your companies, which initially marched in lock step, are now kicking sand in each other's faces. It isn't long before someone decides to walk away from the relationship.

It doesn't matter what kind of customers you have. Monetarily marginal or sound as a dollar, one thing is certain: purchasing relationships will have their ups and downs. If you don't want to go down with the shipments, you'll have to keep up with the credit times.

Customer Types

Problem customers come in all shapes and sizes, and all customers are inherently equipped with one of two separate, but sizeable, challenges:

1. The customer is not likely to pay its invoices on time and/or in full (the customer is a marginal one) or

2. The customer is likely to pay its invoices on time and in full (it is currently sound) unless something changes. If a supplier is lulled into complacency by a customer's current soundness, it won't hear that things are going radically wrong. That is, until it is too late.

In other words, every customer—whether it appears sound or marginal—is a potential source of credit and collection problems. Yesterday's marginal/magnificent credit record doesn't pay today's (or tomorrow's) invoice.

It should come as no surprise that the Category #1 customer, the sound customer, is one that salespeople seldom hear about. Why? For three reasons:

1. There are so few truly sound customers. Credit departments are designed to be most responsive to the average customer and, unfortunately, this customer has a marginal credit record. It's tempting to say that the average customer has a below-average credit record.

The problem with this approach: Because there are few sound customers, and they create few problems, they may be foolishly ignored. That is, until an individual customer's crisis is too big to be ignored.

2. Because of their excellent credit histories, sound customers are not monitored as closely as their marginal counterparts. The good risks

don't get a good deal of scrutiny. The credit department assumes they don't need it.

The problem with this approach: While credit history is a good indication of how a customer will handle credit in the future, it is merely that—an indication. An inclination. Not a confirmation. A sound company that goes off the deep end financially often goes deeply into debt before its suppliers even realize that there is a problem. They don't see the problem coming because they aren't looking.

3. Nobody worries about a sound company until it turns into a Category #1, a marginal customer. Of course, by then it's too late to avoid a loss of trust, collection contacts, uncomfortable new credit restrictions, etc.

The problem with this approach: Reversals of fortune are, unfortunately, a common occurrence. They should be anticipated, not depreciated. As noted earlier, yesterday's sound account could easily be today's gone aground account.

Consider what happened in the late 1980s in the computer industry. Two hot-and-heavy hitters—Wang and Prime, companies that were leaders in their field—hit the ground, knocked out cold. Their suppliers, companies that once knocked themselves out to service the debt-torn duo, were also knocked for a loop. Had these suppliers kept their eye on the future, and not the past, they might have spared themselves some heavy losses.

As another example, consider the stock market. Solid-gold stocks that sold for $25 or $30 per share two years ago may be selling for $15 per share today. What does that tell you about a company's value? Or its future? Or the future of its unpaid invoices?

Unfortunately, this inattention to sound customers makes it less likely that you (or your credit department) will sound the credit crisis alarm before it's too late. For example, let's say your company, Company X, runs a pre-credit check on Company A and finds that A has an excellent credit record, excellent credit references and is in excellent financial condition. You quickly offer Company A an extensive credit line. It sounds like the right thing to do.

Unfortunately, because of A's sound reputation (and initial good payment habits), you and your credit department don't keep your ears to the ground. Neither of you hears the loud-and-clear reference rumblings that indicate a significant and negative change in A's creditworthiness.

You continue to sell materials to A on credit. Since its purchases are unabated ("we'll keep selling to them because they've always been good for it"), the account balance is quickly escalated. Suddenly, you find that A is no longer a customer-in-good-standing, it is a customer-in-a-good-deal-of-debt. Had you or your credit department honestly monitored A in behavior/payment/track record terms, the situation might have been avoided.[34]

Ironically, the Category #1 customers (the marginals) create fewer cataclysmic collection crises because they are initially tagged as "potential problems." Take the case of Customer Y. You knew from the beginning that if you did business together it would be an iffy situation due to Y's spotty credit record.

Y will never owe your company a great deal of money because it has been given very little lending leeway. Maybe its credit line is only good for half a month's materials, or it is being restrained by a "15 day net" net. Perhaps it must clear all previous purchase payments before posting a present P.O. You can bet that your credit department consistently monitors Y's purchasing and payment behavior (Are the order sizes/specs changing? Are invoices paid out of order? Is Y making partial payments? Is the check late?). In short, there's no chance that Y will do anything radically wrong because your credit department isn't going to give it the chance. Y is a reined-in risk.

Bottomline: No credit account—not the "sounds good" or the "sounds good enough"—can be taken for granted. As soon as an account is taken for granted you could be taken for a ride. All accounts need to be checked periodically for credit problems and monitored continuously for symptomatic signs (such as major changes in purchasing/payment behavior, changes in management/purchasing personnel, etc.). If you and your credit department do that, you can avoid most credit problems.

The Problem Avoidance Program

While you can avoid most credit problems, there is no way you can completely avoid them all. However, there are guidelines available for

[34] If you think that sound customers will be offended by constant monitoring, think again. Think customer service. Think salesmanship. Simply explain to your customers that your credit department continuously monitors their progress so that you can offer them better credit terms, and bigger lines of credit, ASAP. The sales pitch: You don't want to take anything away. You want to give your customers as much as possible, as soon as possible.

the salesperson who is trying to minimize the risks inherent in credit customers—both marginal and seemingly sound.

Note: Many of the following points should sound familiar. After all, they are similar to those guidelines provided for dealing with prospects. Why the parallel? Because customers and prospects are basically the same thing. The main difference between them is that you have a credit history with one and a credit mystery with the other. They both come with risks.

The danger signs you look for in prospects will also appear in present, soon-to-be-problem purchasers. That's why you should treat both parties, more or less, in the same scrutinizing way. The programs, processes and procedures that work for prospects will—with a little work—also work for marginal and sound customers.

Points to Remember in Dealing With Current Credit Customers

The following information, in addition to those points provided in our aforementioned prospect program, should prove helpful in dealing with current credit customers.

• **Know the complete role of the salesperson.** Do you know exactly what you, the salesperson, should do in the event of a payment problem?

There is no universal answer to this question. After all, companies come in a wide range of personalities. As a result, they have a variety of needs, wants and styles. Nowhere is this more apparent than when it comes to collecting past due accounts.

There are two absolutes that credit-granting companies cling to. The first absolute is this: All firms will expect their salespeople to forward any debtor-damaging information they may find. If you are aware, for example, that Customer Q is overextended, underfinanced, or caught between a rock and a hard-up-for-money place, it's your responsibility to pass this information on to the credit department. You are the credit department's eyes and ears; you may be the first to see or hear telltale signs of trouble. You must also be the first to pass it on.

Remember: All customers—particularly those of a marginal make—change over time. Sometimes over a short time. You must be alert to the crumbling credit signs discussed in Chapter 2. Today's credit customer can easily become tomorrow's collection crisis unless you do what you can to stop it.

The second absolute is that no company will expect you to handle credit situations yourself. It would be difficult, if not impossible, for a single salesperson to know everything there is to know about collections (especially collection law) or about his or her customers. Just as it's your job to pass credit crisis signs on to the credit department, it's the credit department's job to feed you overdue invoice information (who holds them, how old they are, how much is due, how critical the problem is, etc.). A salesperson cannot be all things to all people, and should not be expected to know all things about all people. That is, not without a lot of credit staff support!

While these two universal standards are helpful, they leave a lot open to interpretation. One big trouble spot involves determining just what it is that a salesperson should do in the event of an overdue invoice.

Companies tend to take one of three basic approaches to this issue. In some firms, salespeople are expected to personally collect past due payments. These companies believe (correctly) that the sale is not complete until the bill is paid; therefore, collecting cash is part of the sales cycle. In other words, it's the salesperson's responsibility. You don't get your check until the company gets its check.

The basic advantage of this approach is that the company is assured of sales support for its credit program. After all, if the salespeople don't actively collect their accounts, they won't collect their commissions. Unfortunately, forcing salespeople to be this collection supportive may prove to be counterproductive. Should a salesperson be spending his or her time collecting new customers or collecting old accounts? What is the best use of the salesperson's time, effort and expertise?

The second approach to the salesperson's role is a middle-of-the-road route. Firms which take this approach see the salesperson's involvement in collections as very limited in terms of time, effort, angst and responsibility. They don't expect salespeople to play all nine collection innings, they just ask them to throw the first payment pitch. If they strike out, well, no problem. The credit department goes to bat with the debtor.

There are major benefits to this limited engagement approach. Salespeople, because they know their customers personally, are more likely than a credit colleague to know what will motivate a quick payment (such as statements of fact, threats or professional pleas). Salespeople are more likely to get their phone calls returned (or forwarded to the proper people) than are credit staffers. Salespeople can collect money while on site, while credit and collection departments are often too far away to express the same blend of convenient urgency. In their unrelenting sales role, salespeople subconsciously communicate that the buyer/supplier relationship is still in the sales (and not just in the collection) stage.

Clearly, this program will ensure a strong cooperative effort between the sales and credit departments. Their respective duties are both clear and clearly understood. However, as a downside, when collection responsibilities are divided, the inherent coordination problems will multiply. The credit department may accidentally make the second collection contact long after (or even worse, *before*) the salesperson has notified the customer. If the salesperson doesn't keep up with the first-round collection calls, a lot of accounts are going to lie around collecting nothing but dust. In short, when departments share a job they also need to share intricate in-depth information about when and how well they are doing it. This requires additional time and effort.

Finally, the third approach a company can take to delegating collection tasks is to have its salespeople do the selling and its credit department do the collecting. In this scenario, no salesperson is expected (or in some cases even allowed) to collect funds or handle any collection communications. Why? Because this company believes that a salesperson who handles collection tasks may suffer a loss of sales.

The major benefit of this third approach is that it takes advantage of job specialization. The sales staff handles all sales, the credit department handles all collection problems. By giving collection tasks to professional payment-prodders (trained personnel who have the time, experience, expertise, resources and power to do the job right), the company should increase its collections.

The cloud that goes with this silver lining is obvious. By removing salespeople from the collection process altogether, there is less pressure on the past-due purchaser. Credit department threats tend to be delivered by phone, letter or attorney, not via face-to-face faceoffs. Arm's length actions from a credit department are easier to ignore than a salesperson at your door.

Note: This third approach also puts less pressure on salespeople. Out from under the burden of any collection duties, some salespeople will push their credit department to accept credit purchases from very high-risk customers. They will promote undeserved special credit terms and unjustifiably high credit limits. Because they see all collection problems being handled by another department, they look past all credit issues and see only $ales.

In summary, there is no one best approach to who should "do the dunning." These is only the approach that works best for your company. Whatever that approach is, it's best that you clearly identify your corporate collection role and learn to roll with its inherent punches.

• **Never *collect* past due payments. *Sell* your customers on the idea of paying their overdue debts.** You aren't a credit and collection specialist; you're a savvy salesperson. Instead of trying to be a collection staff member—something which you are not—why don't you leverage your special sales strengths?

It's true, you can't force customers to pay their bills. Nobody can. You can, however, make a customer want to pay you.[35] How? By stressing the numerous quantitative and qualitative benefits available to those who pay their bills on time and in full. For example:

• Customers who pay their bills promptly save money via fast-pay discounts. As discussed in the last chapter, companies that utilize fast-pay discounts can save double-digit dollars. That's because fast-pay discounts are a no-risk, high-yield investment.

• Customers who don't pay their initial bills may end up paying their original invoice plus interest or finance charges, legal or collection fees, court costs, etc. If the customer doesn't like paying its $1000 invoice, how would it feel paying an additional $100 in finance charges plus $500 in attorney and court fees? Bad payment behavior doesn't pay: it *costs*.

• Customers who pay their bills on time receive their suppliers' best credit terms and highest possible lines of credit. Your company isn't going to bet its profit margin on customers with a marginal credit record. Top credit terms and high credit limits are a reward for good behavior.

---

[35] Know your competition. Your past-due purchaser may not be the real payment problem. The actual debt dilemma could be a function of the customer's other suppliers, the companies that are competing with you for the buyer's limited cash.

If this is the case, simply demonstrate to the debtor why paying your bills makes more sense that paying other invoices. You may have a better fast-pay discount, higher interest/finance charges, a more determined credit department, a more critical product or closer ties to credit reporting bureaus.

• Customers who pay their bills promptly keep their good credit records (i.e., negative information won't be forwarded to national credit reporting companies, regional credit bureaus, or local credit co-operatives). Good credit records are important because they help buyers line up new or expanded lines of credit. He who snubs a supplier today, eventually will have to pay.

• Customers who pay their bills on time develop a list of good credit references (good for signing up new suppliers or bank financing). Suppliers can sell more than just their products. They can also sell other suppliers on a customer's creditworthiness.

• Customers who pay their bills on time and in full avoid the hassle, embarrassment and long-term repercussions of having a collection agency action on their credit record. Such actions never leave a debtor's credit record, and they are there for all potential suppliers to see.

• Customers who pay their bills in accordance with your credit terms can continue to be your customers. You can keep giving them "convenient access to top quality goods at the lowest possible price." Remember: Getting your product—not getting into debt—is why they became your customers in the first place.

It's the way of the business world: Suppliers go out of their way for outstanding purchasers, not out-of-money purchasers. Money talks.

Customers have to be sold on the idea of paying their invoices, just as they have to be sold on the idea of purchasing your products. That's why the best way to present collection problems is to package them as profit opportunities.[36] Think and act optimistically, not pessimistically.

---

[36] Ensure that your debtor has to face the music, but also give ways to save face. Your initial collection comments should include "ways out." For example:

• If you've lost your copy of the invoice, I have one right here. I can even wait while you process the payment.

• It's possible the check crossed—or was lost—in the mail. Let me call the accounts receivable department. If they don't have the check yet, why don't you put a stop pay order on it and cut us a second one? That way, you know any possible problem is taken care of. One less thing for you to worry about!

• Was there some problem with the shipment that affected the invoice total? If an adjustment needs to be made to the bill, let's get it taken care of right away. That way, we can process any other orders you may need without this hanging over our heads.

You should also sell yourself on the idea of collecting past due payments. Remember that:

• Quick collection actions make it easier for a past-due customer to pay in full. Don't want until a customer is $50,000 in debt; collect the $10,000 monthly balance on a monthly basis. That way cutting the check won't cut so deeply into one month's money.

• Collecting past due payments makes it easier for you to make a sale. Past due purchasers often don't place new credit orders for fear that they would be rejected. In addition, customers who are continually past due (not just with you but with other companies as well) are most likely to take their business where they don't have to take major collection flack. Keep their accounts current, and you'll keep them as current customers.

• When you collect your past due accounts, you know how the interface is handled. You needn't worry or wonder about how things went.

• **Contact your customer immediately when there is a problem—when a payment is past due or a credit purchase can't be processed.** Don't compound the late payment/purchasing error with a late collection response. That just makes things go from bad to worse.

Give your collection-caused communiques the same immediate attention you give your hot sales leads. If you don't, you'll lead yourself—and your company—into fiscal hot water.

The older an invoice is, the lower its collectability and monetary value. In essence, time is money. Wasting time once a debt is due causes that debt to lose value.

That's bad enough, but there are other collection-critical corollaries at work. For example, the older an invoice...

...the more difficult it is to deal with it rationally, pleasantly and efficiently. This applies to both the buyer and the supplier.

As a supplier, are you more concerned about an invoice that's one day or one month overdue? As a buyer, are you more embarrassed by a debt that's four days or four months old?

...the more pressure your company will apply to collect it. Unfortunately, when you push a customer for payment, you may push him into your competitor's camp.

Assume that you are responsible for both collecting past due debts and collecting sales. If your company is pressuring you to collect an age-old invoice—and if that becomes your primary goal—the delinquent debtor is going to walk. It will take its business someplace where buyer needs are more important than supplier needs (your need to collect the debt).

...the less likely it is that you can process the customer's present purchase orders. Your sales will suffer, as will your company's revenues.

If Firm F has a past due debt of $10,000 with your company, it's not presently in the position to order more merchandise. In fact, it won't be slated for more deliveries until it has a clean debt slate. Unfortunately, this may also give your customer another reason to throw its purchasing weight behind one of your competitors.

Collection calls need to be made in a time-effective manner, when you are dealing with a minor inconvenience rather than a major complication. If you can't make your collection calls in a timely manner, at least take the time to let your credit department know. Let it do the dirty work.

If you are told that a specific order from a referral customer (one whose every credit order must be scrutinized before it is accepted) cannot be processed due to either internal or external problems,[37] tell the customer. ASAP.

Customers assume that once a purchase order is done on paper the purchase is done in fact. They don't think about it anymore; they just think about what they will do with the shipment once it arrives. If it doesn't arrive, that one unprocessed order can create serious disorder.

Assume that Business B places an order with your company. B might have big plans for this purchase. It may be basing an entire advertising campaign, manufacturing cycle or product design around these materials. It may have made delivery or development promises to its customers based on your product's promised delivery date. It may have burned its buying bridges to a prior supplier. In short, it may be putting its faith (and its business future) in your hands, and it may now be in trouble.

If your company cannot or will not accept the credit order, you can't keep Business B in the dark. You need to let it know immediately that the purchase isn't being processed. If you don't, you could incite business problems, ignite hostilities in the customer and perhaps invite a lawsuit. And, ultimately, you will turn a sad situation into a "made them mad" situation. Customers have as much right to know their credit position as you do.

Note: If you have to, send your credit-cancelled customer to a competitor. Do it with a smile. It's better to ruin a good buyer/supplier relationship than it is to ruin that customer for good. Besides, if you treat the customer right, it may come right back.

• **Let the credit department know when a customer's late payment is the result of a legitimate extenuating circumstance.** When invoice amounts or billing information is wrong, customers cannot be expected to pay on time.

Some "payment problems" aren't really collection crises. Often, something else has gone wrong, something that needs to be set right before the customer will pay its bill. Perhaps the customer is withholding payment because:

---

[37] Remember, reasons for refusing to extend additional credit can come from the buyer's or supplier's side of the equation. Perhaps the customer doesn't deserve any more credit; perhaps the company can't afford to extend it. Either way, if your company has denied credit to a company, you can't ignore it. Your customer should be the first (after you) to know. And it must know now.

• it has some type of allowance claim pending (why should your customer pay $500 on invoice #101 when your company still owes it $600 as a function of invoice #100?)

• it hasn't received the shipment yet (most companies won't pay for still-in-the-mail merchandise, fearing their shipment may have disappeared during delivery)

• the merchandise was received after the specified acceptable arrival date (the widgets arrived too late for Company C's Widgets Sale, so C no longer will accept them)

• the merchandise was misrouted (the customer can't find the merchandise, so it won't pay you)

• the customer received the wrong merchandise (companies don't mind getting what they pay for, but they do mind paying for what they don't want to get)

• your company mailed only a partial shipment

• the order was accidentally duplicated (doubling orders leads to double trouble: delivery difficulties and payment problems)

• the order was overshipped and the customer had no place to put it (the customer isn't going to pay you for creating inventory adversities)

• some or all of the merchandise was damaged in transit or defectively manufactured (if the merchandise isn't useable, there's no use expecting the customer to pay for it)

• the merchandise was refused without being reviewed and then returned (if your customer didn't keep the merchandise, you can't keep asking it for payment)

• the shipment was billed to the wrong company/department or the invoice contained the wrong prices, quantities, credit terms, etc. (the customer isn't going to pay you right away because it doesn't know the right amount to pay).

Any of these extenuating circumstances is a legitimate excuse for a late payment. There's no need to make a federal case out of it because after all, your company may be the one at fault. Take each case under advisement. Immediately inform your credit department of the problem and do what you can to get it solved. Once the correction is made, the outstanding bill can be paid (if possible, the customer should be allowed to access the fast-pay discount).

Note: Another reason to immediately address extenuating circumstances is that once you fix the problem, you nix subsequent ones.

Of course, if the amended invoice doesn't immediately generate the intended payment, the niceties are ended and collection efforts must be expended.

• **Don't let customers abuse your terms of sale.** This includes net payment dates (the maximum time that a company has in which to pay its bills), fast-pay discounts, interest or finance charges, and special credit terms.

Back when Customer K was still just a prospect, you introduced it to your credit conditions. The net due date. The fast-pay discount. The interest/finance charges on past due accounts. Any special credit terms that applied. Remember? You carefully walked that customer through what these terms were and what they meant, where they applied and how they worked. There's no doubt this customer knew what it was getting into.

What's more, one of Customer K's purchasing principals offhandedly "initialled off" on your credit conditions on the signed credit application form (which, with your corporate counter signature, immediately transformed it into a credit contract). With that, the principal pointedly promised that Customer K would fulfill, in full, the conditions of the contract. Including, but not limited to, the payment conditions.

If things are headed downhill (except for K's past dues, which are on the upswing), you must assertively but politely remind it (both verbally and in writing) that its purchasing contract requires that all payments be made in accordance with your terms of sale. No ifs, ands, or buts.[38] This means that payments will be made in full prior to the net date, all fast-pay discounts will meet their timely terms, all finance/interest charges will be paid in full, and all special credit criteria will be met. Period.

Note: It is particularly important that special term customers be kept current. You've given them a financial break, one that could potentially break your bank. Don't let them repay the credit favor with a credit crisis. Remember, they represent your biggest business risk, both as a current customer and as a past due debtor. They owe you more than mere money.

You should always give your collection-case customers a chance to save face, but face it: a contract is a contract. A business can either do

[38] The only acceptable "if, and, or but" would be in the case of extenuating circumstances. However, this is not truly a violation of one's credit contract. A customer can't pay in full and on time if there's some question as to how much is owed and/or when it is due.

as it has promised or it can undo—through past dues—its credit reputation and financial future. There are no other options.

• **Stress the service component of the credit formula.** Your credit and collection department can do more than offer credit—it can proffer professional credit assistance to the credit-confused customer.

If you think your credit department's major function is to turn down customers, think again. It can also educate and assist problem purchasers free of charge. It's a win/win situation. The credit department gains additional customer knowledge. You log additional sales. Your company benefits by strengthening purchase loyalties and earning customer gratitude. And, finally, the customer profits from the use of your credit department's knowledge and expertise.

Your credit specialists can give an array of free support services to any needy credit customers. Customers commonly ask for help with:

• **Financial analysis.** By comparing a customer's sinking current or quick ratios to the ratios of others in the industry, your credit department can tell it where (and perhaps even why) it is out of sync. Identifying a problem area is often half the bottomline battle.

• **Cash flow control.** Your credit department can analyze a customer's credit terms and help it identify ways to increase cash flow (how to utilize net due dates, fast-pay discounts, interest or finance charges to prompt payments). It can also show your customer how to effectively manage outflow (pursuing leases instead of outright purchases, accessing fast-pay discounts, eliminating inventory overages, etc.).

• **Credit references.** Your credit department can show a company how to build a solid credit reputation with its suppliers and how to leverage that reputation in future financial dealings.

• **Loan referrals.** Your credit department may be aware of other companies or lending institutions that would be willing to extend credit or lend money to the buyer.

In short, your credit department can help you identify risky customers, thereby removing some of the risk involved in credit transactions.

Credit staff members can also accompany you on sales calls, helping you build rapport and confidence. On-site credit calls can improve a customer's perception of your credit department's professional ability. On-site visits facilitate personal relationships that come in handy when invoices come due. By building a customer/credit interface, your credit department can take pressure off any future credit situation. In short, credit staffers can meet with customers when there's good will, instead of just when there's a problem.

Used properly, credit is the ultimate support service. Credit supports both customers and salespeople because credit makes it possible for customers to buy and salespeople to sell. In other words, credit helps you do your job.

In summary, don't worry about whether or not a current customer is defined as "sound." In the long run, it doesn't matter. Since things change constantly, they can always change for the worse. You must be prepared.

If there's one secret to dealing effectively with current credit customers it is this: treat them like sales prospects. As noted earlier, the only difference, credit-wise, between a customer and a prospect is that you have first-hand experience with the former and only second-hand tales of the latter.

Sound and marginal customers both deserve your ongoing attention, both in terms of sales and in terms of credit. Be mindful of the "marginals," scrutinize the "sounds."

Chapter 4

The Credit Department's Contribution

No doubt you've noticed: This book talks about teamwork between the credit and sales departments but, so far, has mostly discussed increasing and strengthening the role of the sales staff. In other words, "teamwork" means that the sales team needs to do more work for the credit staff. Right?

You'll be pleased to learn that this chapter promotes a completely different perspective. It's time to discuss the Salesperson's Bill of Credit and Collection Rights. This Bill of Rights consists of the support services you have a right to expect from your credit department.

The Salesperson's Bill of Credit and Collection Rights

Your credit department will...

...do everything in its power to process every dollar of profitable[39] sales.

---

[39] By definition, a sale is profitable if its related revenues are higher than its related expenses. Because it is difficult to predict the revenues related to a specific sale (Will the customer pay in full? Will it use the fast-pay discount or have to pay finance charges?) and the expenses related to a particular purchase (everything from basic manufacturing and shipping costs to related collection/tax/financing/etc. expenses) it can also be difficult to separate the profitable purchases from red-ink-inducing revenues.

A full-fledged credit investigation (complete with credit reports, reference checks, financial reviews, and worst case scenario analyses) isn't cheap, but it is priceless. To you, to your credit department, and to your marginal or sound prospect or customer.

If your credit department is able to make pre-sales (prospect) and ongoing (current customer) credit checks, it should be able to offer at least minimal credit to most businesses. These credit lines may come with strings attached (personal guarantees, a bank's standby line-of-credit, pledged collateral, etc.), but at least they come through. And, as a result, so will your sales.

Your credit department will...

...investigate all prospects/customers with an open mind. Keep in mind that because companies continuously change, your credit staff has just cause to maintain its monitoring.

...diagnose potential problems in individual prospects and customers. For prospects this means a bad payment record or poor business references; for buyers, slower payments, increasing customer claims, an impending insolvency, etc.

...recognize that in many cases, these potential credit problems can be prevented or circumvented via cautious credit conditions (the aforementioned "strings").

...your credit department will develop a collection approach that simultaneously collects cash, reduces risk and enhances customer relations.

If you think that balancing your customers' and company's needs is difficult, try juggling cashflow, credit risk and customer relations all at the same time. Speed and tact are the keys to this juggling act. By collecting cash quickly, the credit department is able to minimize risk (the older the account, the less collectable it is) and maintain good customer relations. Customers are easier to deal with: (1) when their past due accounts are no big deal (not too old and not too big) and (2) if they are approached before past due problems negatively affect present-day purchasing.

Your credit department will...

...immediately identify overdue invoices (thanks to computers, this task is now relatively easy and error free).

...immediately move to collect all past due accounts. As one credit manager puts it: "He who hesitates, it costs!"

...pursue procrastinated payments with the greatest possible tact. Your credit department will give any customer a chance to save face and/or avoid long-term credit record repercussions.

...provide counseling or education services to those customers who will profit from them. Translation: Your credit department will help customers improve their bottomline which will, in turn, improve your own profit picture.

When it comes to problem customers, your credit department would rather educate than litigate and would rather provide assistance than face resistance. That's why most credit departments are happy to provide your customers with free financial/cash flow analysis, credit references, and/or referrals (relative to loans, A/R factoring, collection services, etc.).

When your credit department helps a customer with its credit crises, it also helps you gain the customer's sales, gratitude, trust and loyalty. In short, you and your company stand to gain both qualitatively and quantitatively.

Your credit department will...

...determine why a customer is in trouble (sometimes a credit armchair quarterback—with an arm's length, objective view—can call the shots better than the firm on the field)

...take the trouble to help a customer extricate itself from the pervasive problem expediently and acceptably (without facing bankruptcy)

...your credit department will maintain open and active communication channels between the sales staff, top management and problem accounts.

The free flow of credit/client information is as important to your credit department as its cash flow. That's why your credit staff will try to keep everyone in the credit picture involved and informed.

Your credit department will..

...let you know what is happening credit-wise with your prospects/customers. This ensures that you are utilizing your time, effort and resources to their best advantage.

...let your customers know what is happening credit-wise with respect to their accounts. A customer's purchasing power—in fact, its entire power grid—is a function of its credit line. After all, it can only sell or work with what it can buy. If a customer is about to experience a power drain or a power surge, it mustn't come as a big shock.

...inform top management of aggregate changes in the company's credit position.[40] Managers need financial information before they can proceed with other revenue-requiring proprietary plans (such as advertising, market-ing, hiring or expansion). Why spend time making plans the company can't afford?

...focus on increasing overall sales and profits, not on its own self-interest or administrative ease.

Credit professionals, like fictitious secret agents, live with danger. High risk accounts and past due payments can make it difficult for the serious staffer to sleep nights.

However, your credit staffers recognize credit's inherent hazards and instead of developing insomnia, develop procedures for minimizing risk while maximizing aggregate corporate profits.

Your credit department will...

...be objective and fair (*really*).

...be willing to take a credit loss, although it will not expose your company to needless bad debt. *Note:* While your credit department can anticipate a certain level of bad debt, it will never use this allowance to accept or justify high risk accounts. Credit will only be extended to those companies that your credit department thinks can and will pay.

...identify flexible credit approaches that will make it possible to extend credit to even the most marginal manufacturers.

...maintain a credit program that reflects both macro (industry or regional) and micro (customer specific) economic conditions.

Developing a strong and mutually supportive relationship between your credit and sales departments is easy. All you have to do is

[40] Credit departments usually provide top managers with a wide range of financial information, thus ensuring that leaders see the corporate credit picture through a wide angle lens. Credit departments commonly send the following to top management: accounts aging reports, days sales outstanding (DSO) information, trend and comparative analyses, information relating to specific problem accounts or write-offs, receivables analysis (an categorization of receivables by degree of risk as segregated/defined by Dun & Bradstreet), analysis of past credit performance by plant/division/geographic/salesperson, etc.

remember that both departments are members of the same corporate team. The common goal is profits; the game plan is cooperation, courtesy and communication. Every position on the team is important. Working together, each unit helps create a whole team greater than the sum of its departmental parts. There are no second string players when team players are the ties that bind a successful business.

❖ ❖ ❖

About NACM

The National Association of Credit Management is comprised of 60 affiliated local associations located throughout the United States, including Alaska, Hawaii and Puerto Rico. These affiliates offer a variety of valuable services to assist in the effective management of their member companies' accounts receivable portfolios. These services include: business collections; industry credit groups; national, regional and local business credit reporting; distressed business services; and a variety of educational seminars and workshops.

Membership in an NACM-affiliated credit association includes membership in the National Association of Credit Management. NACM is a member-owned and controlled organization. Its 36,000 members are credit and financial professionals primarily representing manufacturers, wholesalers, financial institutions and service organizations.

The basic goal of NACM is to increase the profit of member companies through more efficient and effective credit management. Key activities which contribute to achieving this basic goal are: providing training through educational programs and annual conferences, seminars and the national convention; improving international credit practices; supporting sound legislation and regulation at both federal and state levels; investigating and preventing fraud; offering government receivables assistance; publishing a national magazine; and offering a library of publications to meet members' reference needs.

For more information, please contact the national office at:

NACM Member Services
8815 Centre Park Drive, Suite 200
Columbia, Maryland 21045-2158
(410) 740-5560